AUTISM AND THE **QUEST FOR FRIENDSHIP**

ECHOES OF ISOLATION

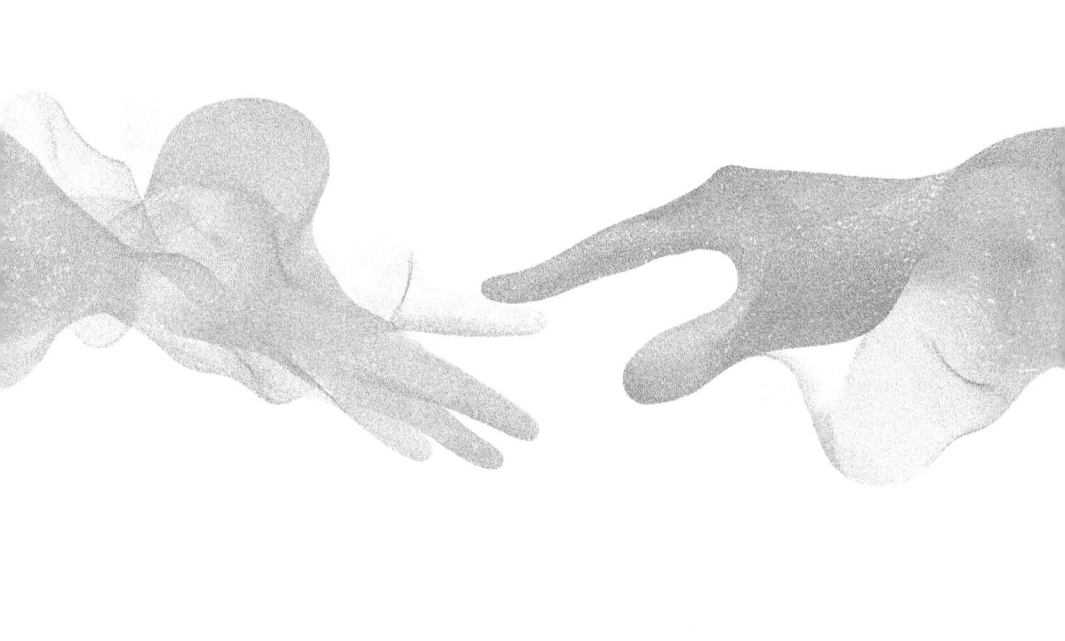

AUTISM AND THE QUEST FOR FRIENDSHIP
ECHOES OF ISOLATION

DIANA P. CATLIN

SALT & PEPPER LEGACY PUBLISHING

Autism and the Quest for Friendship
Echoes of Isolation
Copyright © 2025 by Diana P. Catlin

All rights reserved, including the right to reproduce distribute, or transmit in any form or by any means.

Except as permitted under the U.S. Copyright Act of 1976, no part of this book may be reproduced, distributed, or transmitted in any form or by any means, or stored in a database or retrieval system without the written permission of the authors, except in the case of brief passages embodied in critical reviews and articles where the title, author and ISBN accompany such review or article.

While all the stories in this book are true, some names and identifying details have been changed or omitted to protect the privacy of the people involved.

For information contact:
authordianapepperdinecatlin@gmail.com

Published by:
Salt & Pepper Legacy Publishing

Cover and interior design by
Francine Platt • Eden Graphics, Inc.

Stock images on cover from istockphoto.com
Credit: aelitta, juliawhite, Sachol Sutto, and Tetiana Garkusha

Dehaka from Star Craft II – Published by Blizzard Entertainment for Microsoft Windows
Aromatouch Technique – developed by Doctor David Hill

Paperback ISBN 979-8-89454-036-8
eBook ISBN 979-8-89454-037-5
Audiobook ISBN 979-8-89454-038-2

Library of Congress Control Number: 2024926601

Manufactured in the United States of America
First Edition

DEDICATED TO:

Benjamin Catlin
the child who taught me how to
understand the rest of my family

*"Everybody is a genius. But if you
judge a fish by its ability to climb a tree, it will
live its whole life believing that it is stupid."*
— Albert Einstein

Because I love
Jamie, Jen, Ben, Em, Na, Nat, Mara, Mel, Miri,
Mai, Crys, Rowan, Rhia, Shell, Owen, Iris, Acie

TABLE OF CONTENTS

Dear Reader... ix
Introduction... 1
The Diagnosis 5

The Top 25 Things I Wish I'd Known 9
HIM: Immediately After My Late Diagnosis
HER: Prior to Marrying Him

    1 – Social Communication Challenges 9
    2 – Difficulty Initiating and Sustaining Conversations 14
    3 – Safe Spaces Are Mandatory 20
    4 – Anxiety is Real – Sometimes Debilitating................ 25
    5 – Sensory Sensitivities/Overload 32
    6 – Special Interests 35
    7 – Difficulty Understanding Social Norms.................. 39
    8 – Emotional and Emotionless 44
    9 – There are No Words for Emotions 48
    10 – Bullying and Social Exclusion...........................50
    11 – Difficulty with Empathy and Perspective-Taking 53
    12 – Autistic Burnout....................................... 59
    13 – Textures Are Evil 64
    14 – Routine Keeps Me Grounded.......................... 68
    15 – We Don't Want to Socialize – and It's OK!.............. 70
    16 – We Don't Understand Humor......................... 73
    17 – Eye Contact is Uncomfortable 75
    18 – Viewing the World From Afar 76
    19 – Authority Issues....................................... 78
    20 – Mental FOG...80
    21 – Caretaker Burnout 88
    22 – Reciprocity 91
    23 – Gullability and Innocence 93
    24 – Privileges are NOT Rights............................. 95
    25 – More Lack of Connection 97

Conclusion 109
Postlude 111

ANGELS IN MY LIFE

There have been many angels in my life. People who have reached out to 'lift up the hands which hang down.' You don't even realize how much your handshake, smile or words of encouragement meant. There are so many to whom I owe so much. I wish I could list you all.

Ryan & Char Holdeman, whose friendship runs deep and true.

Deb Mouett, with her sons Dyllon and Dustin Arenivar—for their unparalleled support of Benjamin during the formative years when he played soccer. You made a world of difference, giving him encouragement, friendship, and words of praise which boosted his self-esteem and empowered his life.

Reggie Ford, Massage Therapist
Vicki Sorensen Barlow
Michelle Proffit Ennis
Judy Turner
Spencer & Alicia Grant
Blake Belnap
Pris Hardy
Mike & Jenni Wilson
Brian & Kaylin James
Michael Jeffs
Beverly & Michael Sorensen
Sharon Allred
Amber Allred
AdriAnne Buller
LaRelia Jones
Paula Baldwin, RIP
Ernie & Barbara Gardner
Terra Loutensock
Ron & Francine Lyndaker
Scheri Morrow

Lori Logue
Kathy Thibodeaux —
    dear friend and author
Susan Corbett
Betsy Maxwell Menlove
Annabel & Norman Petty
Taylor Douglas
David Woods
Miranda McGraw
Anita Norris
Meg Condie
Shirley Solomon
Danielle Appling
Doreen Wooley
Orry Albertson
Heather Chandler
Tiffney Christiansen
Wayne & Christine James
Rebecca & Karl Mortensen
Karyn Lynn Grant

Dear Reader,

THERE IS A DEEP and complex reality that comes with loving someone whose communication style differs so profoundly from yours.

I had never heard the term "Autism" or "Asperger's" until the early 2000's. During my time as a mentor and homeschool teacher for my own children and various nephews, nieces, and step-relatives, I became acquainted with many things. My beloved Aunt Barbara handed me an article about autism as I tutored her grandson, and thus began my journey, gently and slowly. I didn't have anyone with autism living in my home at that time.

This didn't last long. Enter, James Catlin and family. Oh, hang on to your hats! My learning curve with autism and other executive processing disorders/mental wiring gone different went from 0.5 to 10 overnight. My education in autism life began with a bang and has definitely been boots-on-the-ground ever since.

My hope is that these reflections will be incredibly valuable to those who may be navigating a similar relationship. These insights are offered to help others feel less alone and more supported, while preparing them for the realities they might face.

– DIANA P. CATLIN

INTRODUCTION

HIM: For this book, I originally thought "Friendless: One Downside of Autism" might be a good title. Then I realized it might be a little too depressing, or perhaps "over the top," and yet it is my reality. You see, until I was about forty-six, I thought I was just socially incompetent. I was in my third marriage, and I only had two friends.

HER: When we married in 2000, I knew nothing about the spectrum. Autism and Asperger's were beginning to be discussed in more public forums, but they hadn't filtered down to my reality. James informed me that some of his children didn't listen well. He described an incident where he was helping one of his daughters clean her room, and he kept pointing to a coin on the floor saying, "There it is, pick that up…" and the child kept bouncing everywhere else in the room, and never did manage to pick up the coin. While I heard this description, and some other horror stories of parenting unresponsive children as a single father, I did not understand. I truly believed that if children were showered with love, things would work out. I still believe this to be true, but when you are mothering neurodivergent children there are depths through which you must wade, with grit and determination. These experiences will challenge your beliefs, your commitment and your self-worth. I had NO idea what I was really getting into.

I had four children, all very much on the gifted scale. He also had four children. I used to tease him that he used his gifted child as bait and then I got to know the others after we were married. Two of our children shared birthdays, which seemed like fate. Our marriage union brought all ten of us together—and it was fun to see *our unique family* had kids ages 8, 9, 10, 11, 12, 13, 15, and 16! The day we married, my son went from three sisters to seven. A few weeks later, we had them meet each other at Disneyland. We were truly blessed that they all blended and behaved much like life-long siblings.

HIM: When we married, I informed Diana that I didn't really know what love was.

HER: Looking back, that was such an understatement. I had no way to quantify how much his 'not knowing what love is' would be a running theme throughout our entire marriage. We had written and talked on the phone for months before we married. He had written a poem for us, using all the children and their traits. We hadn't met yet, but our conversations shared a lot, and poetry was a creative outlet for James. It went straight to my "Aaahhh!" emotions. I did not realize at the time that it wasn't the same for him. After we married and there were now eight children, he pretty much disappeared from our lives—in SO many ways. Emotionally, he evaporated, and he wasn't physically "present" either. I didn't yet know that this was not the appropriate way to describe this scenario. He didn't "evaporate emotionally" after the marriage. He had *never* been emotionally attached to it in the first place. Not like I was.

HIM: Friendship looks complex and challenging to me. It feels scary and nerve-wracking with potholes everywhere. I've watched neuro-typical acquaintances, and my children navigate the challenges of social interaction, learning to communicate, to forgive (thanks to my wife), and figure out social cues, or how to 'read a room.' I struggle. It makes it nearly impossible for me to form, much less maintain friendships. Due to this 'disconnect,' my relationship with Diana suffers.

THE DIAGNOSIS

HIM: In roughly 2010 there was a lot going on. The girls were dating. The kids were in school. Some were planning marriages sooner or later. My marriage was feeling rocky and disconnected. Whenever Diana would ask for time with me, or to go somewhere on a date, I would tell her she should go out with some of her other friends. This was not a good time in my own brain. I was spiraling in a vortex of my own mental anxiety coupled with severe depression, further complicated by my bipolar issues, and I was also on medication that was messing with my body systems. I was so lost, swamped in my own chaos. I did not realize how serious it was.

Diana needed me, and I simply wasn't available in any way. Sadly, even on my best days, I don't comprehend the necessary social-emotional connections or communication that would benefit a relationship. I forget conversations within moments, and in addition to that I was deliberately shutting her out. At this time, our youngest was diagnosed with autism in the school system as well as by a physician. Another daughter was also diagnosed.

HER: When Ben was diagnosed with Asperger's syndrome (before it was all rolled up under the autism umbrella), I began a journey into the absolute unknown. Until this time, the other siblings with learning difficulties, Jen and Nat, had been labeled at school as 'learning disabled, disorder NOS.'

How I had come to hate that NOS label, which meant 'not otherwise specified.' I struggled with that for years. *How can I work with it, if there is nothing specific to target?* I felt like I was flying blind, and there were no solutions or education to help me navigate. I desperately needed a light-bulb illumination moment, a map, a mentor, something! And during the last several years I had been and still was bitterly hurt that I was all alone in this struggle. James had 'checked out' a long time ago.

One of the teachers at the elementary school was very, very helpful. She led me through the murky waters, helping to shed light on the process of understanding our son. When I saw the typical responses to the questions on the exam for those on the spectrum, my first thoughts were not about Ben.

But that's James! And then I read the next question. *Oh, wow! And that's James too!* I felt like I had fallen into a pool of enlightenment. I knew James needed to take this test. I just knew it. For me, *so* much of what was *wrong* with my life began to make sense.

HIM: Diana asked me to take the test, hoping it might help us both. I told her I would, that it wouldn't be a problem. However, when I began to do so, anxiety struck and I began to have trouble breathing. I was scared. I turned to her and asked, "What if I answer a question wrong? What if I don't get it?"

HER: I remember James' terror at taking this *exam*. I remember telling him it wasn't really an exam, and there weren't any right or wrong answers. This was a tool to help us discover new information, to confirm certain behaviors or traits we simply hadn't pinpointed yet. He was able to calm his breathing and distress enough to simply answer the questions. That in and of itself, was a milestone.

Long story short, we were sitting in our small office space

at home, knee to knee. I looked at him and said, "James, these results show that you are autistic, there is *no* question about it. You are smack-dab in the center of all the diagnostic numbers." I remember he looked at me for what felt like a long time, and then his face crumpled as he toppled over onto my lap and began to sob like someone who was lost. He cried out, "Is *this* why I don't understand so many things? Is *this* why I'm so confused? Is *this* why I don't have any friends? Is *this* why humor escapes me?" And he shook and cried his sorrow and soul-deep anguish into my arms. I just held him.

HIM: As I read the results it was like someone had turned a light on in a dark room. Thus began my journey of self-analysis instead of just accepting that I was stupid or narcissistic, neurotic, or crazy. I remember thinking, *Is this really why I am like I am?*

THE **TOP 25 THINGS**
I WISH I'D KNOWN

HIM: Immediately After My Late Diagnosis
HER: Prior to Marrying Him

Following are 25 things that may be helpful for neurotypical (NT), non-autistic individuals to be aware of when interacting with neurodivergence, and vice versa. The format begins with a stated challenge, followed by experiences and insights.

1 Social Communication Challenges

CHALLENGE: Autistic individuals may struggle with understanding *non-verbal* cues such as: body language, facial expressions, and tone of voice, which are crucial for building and maintaining normal friendships, both personal and professional.

HIM: This area is my proverbial Achilles' heel. I'm going to state it straight up for you from my personal experience. This is one area of potential trauma, severe stress, anxiety, meltdown, or complete shutdown just waiting to happen.

Have you ever been reprimanded in the workplace, or disciplined at school, or told in social situations that you've just been way too rude, too blunt, too *something*? Have you been told that you have no tact, you are not a team player, or you've used an inappropriate tone of voice? That you're being too loud?

Here's the straight of it. I don't understand tone of voice, pace, volume, verbal, non-verbal, or body language. This is not even a thing! When I walk into a room, it's me, the room, the people, and my anxiety is holding me together. I don't *get* the whole *tone* thing.

Pause for a moment, please take in a breath… Please, hear me again. *I don't get this part of life.* I have tried, taken classes, and talked with my wife. I simply don't get it. I haven't been able to *fix* the problem, or re-wire it. I am just the way I am. This is not a cop-out, an avoidance issue, or a lie. I've watered my pillow at night in utter distress accompanied by feelings of failure for this 'defect.'

Let's continue. What does 'inappropriate tone' even mean? I try to communicate, it doesn't come out right, yet I don't recognize there has been a faux pas. I'm not even aware that something different is needed or required. This is the huge, often overlooked elephant in the room between 'typical' and 'divergent.'

HER: Ultimately, this is where awareness, kindness, and understanding come into play. Only these things can diffuse a situation. When a 'typical' converses, they frequently have the ability to portray the desired message. When a 'divergent' (ND) receives the message and responds, be prepared for the likely possibility that they've gotten it wrong, even though you were patient, calm and careful in your efforts. Communication between NT and ND takes work, lots of work, generously sprinkled with sugar, every day.

HIM: When someone asks me, "Why are you raising your voice?" I'll say, "I'm not…" My voice might have gone up a bit, but I may have just been trying to convey a message, or feel I'm not being heard so my voice gets more intense, but none of this is conscious. I didn't mean to be. It just means this is how I function in conversation. If you'll listen to my words, you may get further. If you're trying to read too much into my tones, which we've already covered, that becomes your perception of things, and definitely not my reality.

This terrible obstacle affects not only my personal relationships, but my professional work life as well. Sometimes we're told, 'Act professional.' We're taught to 'mask up' in a certain way. Have you taken those job interview skill classes? They try to teach us to sit a certain way, to respond in a certain way, with just the right amount of fact, tact and humor. I could never get it right.

For most of us, this ideal is an impossibility. 'Behaving professionally' isn't a thing, though I must admit I have tried, and will continue to try. But I can tell you that after more than forty years in workplaces, and failed social situations, that these things are unachievable by your average autistic person. *Tact* ranks right up there with *tone* and humor. Not gonna happen.

HER: I find this assessment to be fairly accurate for him. 'Professionalism' in the typical sense is a tough fit for many autistic individuals. All the unspoken rules around tone, humor, and tact often feel like an impossible maze; a puzzle with no solution. The pressure and perceived need to conform, to blend in especially when emotions, jokes, innuendo, and a host of other body language clues don't come naturally, leads to frustration, miscommunication, and an overload on the mental and emotional systems in the body.

Taking that reality into the realm of marriage is equally traumatizing, eventually, for both parties.

We carry soul-deep expectations into the marriage relationship. We believe that growth will be mutual, that compromise will happen naturally and that we can 'meet in the middle.' It's so deep we don't even articulate, it simply *is*. But all this can be turned on its head when one partner's abilities and neurotype don't align with our assumptions, beliefs and neural wiring. It's so hard to wrap one's head around the differences.

For nearly two decades I kept thinking, *if I just have enough patience, he'll learn, grow, and improve his communication skills. That's how it works in a loving marriage, right?* We're supposed to grow into it, learn together, and become better, together. Hmmm, not so much.

On the one hand, it was so much easier to have a relationship when we just spoke on the phone before we married. After twenty plus years, I'm so frustrated. It appears the type of growth I kept hoping for will never occur. Why?! The give-and-take and compromise I imagined has never materialized and the weight of needing to redefine what communication, growth, and connection will look like in our marriage feels like an isolating, heavy burden. The obvious conclusion is, it won't be us 'growing together' nearly as much as it will be *Me* needing to adapt, to fit a different, unexpected paradigm. He is rigid, fixed, immovable, and ultimately unaware how much it hurts. I don't like it, this isn't normal. Yet, this *is* my new 'normal.' This is horrendously difficult.

There are more questions that go deeply beyond the surface. I keep asking myself, *How do I clarify this for me? I seem to be the only one really concerned with this dilemma. How do I make sense of the imbalance without losing myself in the process? And what does love and acceptance look like now? And...will it ever look and feel like a relationship I would be happy to remain in?*

Well, the 'normal' I envisioned doesn't exist here, it never did. It was in my mind. And yet the sorrow over this 'failure' is tragically painful and real. Do my efforts even matter when I'm the only one concerned with this? Yes, it matters. I'm completely reshaping what communication and connection mean in an NT-ND relationship, even though it feels so completely unbalanced right now.

The reality is that those with autism simply don't fit the 'average' mold for social expectations, no matter how hard they try, or don't try and don't seem to care either. This may lead both parties to heightened anxiety, overwhelm, depression and meltdown. In fact, over and above the depression I've seen wreak havoc on my spouse has been the final insult of autistic burnout. (discussed in chapter 12)

HIM: During the last sixty years I have learned to fake things. It's one of the reasons that initially, some people think I'm not autistic. This brings with it another unexpected dilemma. The problem and cost of putting on a fake facade for anyone else is increased stress, extreme mental fatigue and a feeling of being disingenuous. The predicament is exacerbated by a lack of all the social facts (which I'll state again, I miss so many of them). Masking is an uncomfortable effort to alter who you are in order to fit in with the herd. It doesn't end well.

HER: James! Tonight, you've done it again. You came by Jen's home and said, 'I'm not staying, but I'm gonna let you know I'm *very* distressed about the changes in my book,' and then you went back home. Your anxiety and irritation were positively dripping off of you. I could *see* it. So, I stopped by your place later in the day. You were still upset. I informed you that your body language had spoken volumes for you this afternoon, in a good way. You responded and said, 'But all I said was that I wasn't going to stay…' That's true, that is all you stated verbally, but your body language spoke so much more. 'But I didn't say anything…' (this is what you 'keyed' on)

Look, Jamie! Just because you can't *read* body language in others, we both know you miss it *all* the time; it doesn't mean you don't *have* body language for other people to read! This NT can see the body language you display and it does affect how I communicate with you. Understanding, awareness, and kindness must go both ways, as stated above.

I'm not asking you to become anyone you're not. I'm asking you to grow (just an itty, bitty bit) and be aware that there are things I see that you don't. There is a *reason* the nurses at the VA told you to shut up and listen to me more often.

INSIGHT: In simplest terms, communication is difficult and frustrating when ND's miss non-verbal body language NT's see; especially when the NDs don't recognize when their own tones/pitch/body-language are inappropriate for the situation. Compassion, awareness and patience are must-have skills for both parties.

2 Difficulty Initiating and Sustaining Conversations

CHALLENGE: Starting and maintaining conversations can be challenging for autistic individuals. We may need help knowing when to speak, what to say, or how to respond appropriately in conversations.

HER: Do you often feel like you're both speaking English, but you're not communicating? His words don't match up with what you think they should mean.

I remember arguing with one of my sisters for years. One day we actually pulled out a thesaurus and a dictionary. Together we figured out that when she was talking she would often use the first definition of a word in the dictionary. By analyzing that same word, we found out I wasn't using the first definition but might be two or three down the list. No wonder we were having communication issues.

I've been told people with Asperger's think visually, not in language like I do. James tells me this is true, for him. If those with average language development, like my sister and I, in a 'normal' or NT family can have the troubles we endured while trying to have a standard conversation; can you imagine the highs and lows that would (and do) occur with typical NT verbal language versus atypical ND imagery, complicated with ND executive processing time which is exponentially slower than mine as an NT? I don't even want to go there! I need an interpreter.

HIM: Speech patterns, for those with autism, vary. I've met some who think really fast, and yet they talk slowly because it's as if there is a barrier not allowing the thought to flow through to the tongue. This can also manifest as a challenge in trying to get our ideas down on paper. I hated English and writing in school. It filled my soul with anguish.

HER: Do you constantly feel shut out? You want to discuss something difficult with them but you get the 'hand in your face' gesture? The neurodivergent are often uncomfortable with dissension and confrontation; and this includes a simple conversation that they perceive as potentially fraught with unseen potholes and tension. This is a common thing.

We have also found that the feelings involved in various conversations greatly enhance or hinder speech patterns. My autistic ND's do not quickly process an opinion that is different than theirs. This is a reality. In fact, they may not ever be able to wrap their head around it. Be prepared for that. Being unable to 'see' life from a different perspective may be permanent. This is part of an 'inflexible brain wiring' pattern. This is where it gets intense, and real.

In our family, we call this interruption of dialogue 'necessary processing time.' I have become skilled in not requiring a conversation to keep galloping along, as per my 'normal wiring.' This is only one way I've learned to adjust my own behavior to better support them. When Jen holds up a hand, or simply looks up and shakes her head, I know it's time to allow her 'processing' the time it needs. Jen wants to share something, and it is kindness to allow her the time to mentally arrange the message so that she can be happy with it.

What kinds of speech patterns are there? The following is by no means an all-inclusive list. We have found many of these in our ND family.

- **Non-verbal**. Those with the more significant challenges in autism may be non-verbal or have minimal speech.

- **Echolalia**. This rare disorder involves repeating words or phrases after you hear them from someone else. It doesn't matter if it's the repetition of a person in the room, or something on the radio. It can happen immediately, or be remembered weeks later, and repeated then. This may begin a conversation, or a request.

- **Palilalia**. This involves involuntarily repeating the words, phrases or sentences they themselves have just spoken. The repeated words are often much less audible, and a bit faster than the originally spoken words. We discovered this speech pattern in our son, Ben.

- **Literal Language**. This is where an individual is wired to understand language only in an absolutely literal way. The points of nuanced humor, jokes, idioms, sarcasm, and figurative language are often completely missed.

    – Their formal and extremely precise use of language may sound unusual, sometimes far too technical for the average conversation.

- **Monotone, or Unusual Prosody** (love this word). All this means is that children may not pick up the variations in pitch, rhythm, or tone (prosody) found in neurotypical speech. You may remember the previous discussion on tone and pace. This one is so difficult. Some have unusual intonation, not staying on the 'correct' pitches, while others may speak in simple monotone. The volume may be atypical, either too loud or too soft.

- **Normal social language follows certain conversation rules** involving taking turns and staying on topic.

  - One Thanksgiving dinner in particular, Ben walked into the dining area. Without so much as a thought for what was going on in the room, he broke into the conversation with someone already in a discussion, and proceeded to talk about how his video game had ended, etc.

  - Ben didn't recognize his need to 'read the room,' to see how he might comfortably interact with others, knowing when or how to properly join a conversation, and not interrupt too abruptly. He was simply existing in his realm, full of joy.

  - Sometimes the ability to 'comfortably interact' is an NT definition the ND simply don't recognize and frankly don't care about. We would be embarrassed if we broke up someone else's conversation, but *not* my son – he doesn't understand it as a problem.

HER: This level of 'oblivious' is *so* hard on me. It began with James, Jen, Nat, and Ben followed years later by Iris, Owen, Mel, Miri, and Ace.

"How can you *not* see that everyone else was already talking? How can you *not* see that it's time to sit and have supper? How can you be so clueless?"

In this instance the real awareness here needs to fall on the rest of us, yes, me specifically. They're wired this way, and I'm not. I can 'see' it and make personal adjustments. Coming to the space where I can actually understand, deep in my own psyche, that it will 'never be a thing' for him (or them) has been my own personal challenge. We still try though.

- **Difficulties interpreting nonverbal cues** such as gestures, body language and facial expressions may also fall under this category.

- **Monologuing.** Properly maintaining a conversation involves give and take, ebb and flow. People with autism often find it challenging to recognize when others are not still engaged in a conversation. They will continue to speak at length about their preferred topic, ignorant of the fact that the other person may have 'glazed over' and is no longer interested.

- **Delayed Language Development**

- **Advanced Vocabulary and Language Skills**

    - At the higher-functioning end of the spectrum, some individuals may have more advanced vocabulary and language skills.

    - **Hyperlexia.** They may use sentences with complex words and ideas beyond their age level due to their deep, focused interest in specific topics. If you've ever experienced one of these amazing children tell you about dinosaurs, or mechanical things, more than you ever knew (or wanted to know). You'll understand what we mean.

HER: I know a young lady who was on a university campus with her mother. She walked up to an administrative assistant and asked when the next class in veterinary science was beginning, and how she might attend. She gave a verbal resume of several books she'd read, and the frog she had dissected. The young lady in question was not yet nine years old, but her knowledge of and passion for science ran deep and real. At the end of it all, it was agreed that she still needed to complete the 3rd grade.

Additionally, many still struggle with social communication at all other levels, in spite of appearing to be 'all together' because of their hyper focus specialty.

- **Idiosyncratic Language**
    - **Made-up words.** Some conversations will be extra challenging when the autistic person uses unique phrases or words, the meaning of which is only known to the individual.
    - Creating new words or using existing words in unusual ways.

HER: This happened repeatedly in our home as Ben began to develop his vocabulary. There was one point where he was talking about 'firewater,' meaning the water that was coming out of the tap, extra hot.

Another family member decided to correct the mis-used colloquialism explaining that it should only be used to describe alcohol so everyone knew exactly, accurately, what was meant historically. Ben was too frustrated with being corrected and misunderstood to properly process the stress. He had simply been playing with words while doing dishes and expressing his desire to use the new word in conversation. The exchange grew quite heated. I can tell you that when an inflexible, feeling threatened, autistic brain and an inflexible OCD brain go to war over a few small words, it is not pretty, and there are no winners. It's been almost a decade and Ben still carries scars from that encounter. The other party involved wonders why he even bothers to remember that. And so, it goes…

INSIGHT: Please note that each individual with autism is unique, and their speech patterns may not fit neatly into these categories (which list is far from inclusive). Some may exhibit a mix of many characteristics, while others may not exhibit any of these at all.

Additionally, we have personally witnessed the truly miraculous growth and development of speech and communication skills over time. Love, acceptance, and patience offered with *no* thought as to an agenda or timeline of 'skills acquired' really makes a difference. Each day is simply a gift from God, a treasure to be explored. Milestones are mastered when the individual is ready. Mind you, while I understand this, I still find it frustrating on many levels because I like measuring things, and evaluating progress, and checking off lists.

3 | Safe Spaces are Mandatory

CHALLENGE: Discomfort, anxiety, awkwardness, or stress around unfamiliar people and places can arise both unexpectedly and predictably. These feelings of unease, fear, or uncertainty can also occur in the comfort of your own home. Safe spaces are essential for those with sensory challenges. Safe spaces vary by age group and require customization.

HER: Anxiety happens in *his* mind before he even walks out the door. Just the act of taking out the trash and reaching for that doorknob can be overwhelming.

HIM: I don't want to go outside, the unknown is out there, and my mental scripts start plaguing me about the myriad of possibilities. Leaving home is stressful and being around people who aren't safe because I don't know them, their intentions, or personality puts me at risk. Will we even like each other? Will there be drama instead? Heck, I have these questions when I'm about to meet up with my own daughters, let alone strangers. My safe space involves working with my hands. My mother introduced me to model building at a very young age, and I've been hooked ever since.

Ideas to Help Create Comfort in Your Creative/Safe Spaces

Children often require small spaces, fuzzy toys or blankets, motion chairs, or surround pods. There is no such thing as a perfect safe space that will cover all autistic persons.

A Bit Younger
- Weighted blankets
  - Blankets like this are amazing.
  - **HIM:** I like it because it feels like a cocoon, a protective shell.
  - Make sure they are weighted for the age and size of your body. A blanket that is too heavy for you (especially a child) can make it hard to breathe.
- Oversized wearable sherpa fleece hoodie
  - Ben's favorite. He'd rather sleep in this than anything else.
- Hanging chairs or swings
- Create a 'cave' out of pillows

- Create a play nook by placing a blanket over a table
    - Day 1-add pillows and books
    - Day 2-change to dolls and blankets
    - Day 3-change to dress-up super-hero items
    - Day 4-change to dolls and medical/rescue toys
    - Day 5-change to cooking pots, pans, bowls, spoons
- Fidget toys
- Building blocks
    - Legos
    - Lincoln logs
    - Anything that matches their 'focus'
- Squishy things
    - Corn starch goo
    - Clay
- Art centers
    - Pencils and paper
    - Paint and brushes

A Bit Older
- Go to your shop or creative, ordered space to be alone
- Dive into a personal project
- Play music at whatever volume you want
- Wood burning tools
- Artistic supplies for your specific craft
- Computers
- Dim the lights
- Something that is 'backlit' can be soothing without the direct glare of the bulb being evident

- Educate yourself
- Become aware of when sensory overload is happening
  - NT: Learn to 'read' your ND
  - ND: Learn to read how anxiety works on you, personally
  - This helps you develop a coping strategy
- Reduce clutter - order can make all the difference

HER: Interestingly, I believe reducing clutter makes all the difference, but my guys rarely notice the difference unless something is in their way. Yes, I mean it. I have trouble believing it every time. How can you not *see* the dish as you walk by? Yet I digress…

HIM: I do not like the term 'safe space.' This makes me feel like I'm still under threat. When the world is too noisy, busy or confusing, I go to my 'creative zone.' This is the place I have control. I organized it. I understand it. I know how to navigate it. I choose the music or the silence. I can choose the project. It lets me organize anew and regenerate. The need to be in the creative zone can last for a matter of hours (rare), to a matter of days or weeks (more likely). To a great extent, I don't find it necessary to be out in a social situation to be fulfilled. When I decide to come out of my creative space, it's because I've reached a point where I think I can handle the world for a moment or two.

HER: I remember two phrases as I was growing up. Once, I was terribly upset by what a schoolmate had said to me. It caused me days of sorrow. Finally, my dad sat me down and said, "Look, Diana, you've really just got to consider the source." Now, I get it. It was just some little 7-year-old kid, a person without filters, manners, training or an education, and therefore not truly of consequence. Someone without experience or credentials. I should not let someone like that ruin my day, what a waste of time. (I smile at this now, in compassion for the little girl that was me.)

My dad's other solution for creating a good life was the phrase "Pick up your bootstraps, girl, and get moving. It's good to keep your hands occupied with meaningful work, even if your mind is out-of-sorts." He was right.

INSIGHT 1: We have found safe spaces to be vital for autistic individuals. They provide a place to decompress, regulate sensory experiences and feel secure in a world that often feels overwhelming. The unpredictability of sensory input—sounds, lights, textures, and even social interactions—can lead to anxiety, meltdowns, or shutdowns. A safe space acts as a buffer, allowing time to retreat, recover, and regain equilibrium. To state it very simply, safe spaces aren't just about physical comfort—they're a cornerstone for emotional and sensory wellbeing.

INSIGHT 2: Not to play devil's advocate here, but there will be times when places rooted in sensory peace simply will not be available. Is there a way to teach a 'catch phrase' or sentence that means it's time to create that space in your mind, and move along? It can be done, yet the child must be mature enough to understand what it means to be in control of one's emotions and choices. I understand this is usually a skill set for an older, more emotionally mature person and might not work easily with a child.

4 Anxiety Is Real – Sometimes Debilitating – Should I Rehearse Something?

Those on the Spectrum May Not Know What Anxiety Is, How It Feels, Or How To Manage It Themselves

CHALLENGE: Persons with autism need a clear routine and schedule. These tools provide predictability which helps to minimize uncertainty and anxiety. Knowing what to expect reduces mental effort. This is a blessing. But how can you manage 'feelings run amok' if you don't know what they are? Or how it manifests in your body, and how it makes you feel? Or what to call them? Or how to identify them? Or the utter shutdown that is followed by sensory overwhelm and your world just becomes too much, creating additional emotional chaos?

There is an enormous need to help those with autism become better educated about emotions and how they actually affect their bodies. Hopefully they can distinguish between those feelings, and being really, really hungry. Yes, that's a thing.

If you're feeling anxious but only think you have a stomach ache, you can't address the issue with any level of emotional intelligence.

HER: My sweet Nat used to get severe tingling sensations in her limbs. They would go numb accompanied by light-headedness, dizziness, and even a pain in her chest so strong it felt like a heart attack. Her irrationality during one of these episodes became so bad that I took her to the hospital and enrolled her in a program. She was scared and uncertain but trusted me. I promised to look after her four children while she was there.

NAT: I have anxiety! Mom, I've learned so much. I didn't know that's what I was feeling. I didn't understand that my skin crawling and my need to turn away from everything and scream was a manifestation of anxiety. Oftentimes I'd sit there and try to reason, trying to make sense of things in my head, but no matter how much I tried to justify or make something that made *no sense*—make sense—there was this war inside of me.

When you don't know what it is, you feel like you're so lost, stuck in anguish and despair, and you reason that it simply must be this way. I didn't know how to dig myself out of this hole.

I didn't understand that I didn't know many emotion words. (Alexithymia-more in chapter nine) I didn't realize I had no words to describe those feelings. I definitely didn't understand how anxiety, distress, and overwhelm are supposed to feel. Who knew they're supposed to be connected in my mind/body balance? Once I learned what it was, it was a whole new view of the world, and I knew I could be happier by taking myself out of a situation that was harmful, so I could forget about it for a while. I could breathe more easily as I created less stressful situations. I'm coping, but I need to have patience with myself, to take care of myself without guilt.

HER: Anxiety/Stress management needs to be multi-faceted. If you've been told:

- Just calm down
- Stop overthinking
- Ignore it, and it will go away
- You just need to be more positive
- Avoid everything that makes you anxious
- It's all in your head
- Toughen up; life is hard

- You should be over this by now
- You're over-reacting
- Take this one supplement; it will fix everything

You have been seriously misled. While there may be a little bit of truth to be found in some of those suggestions, they are not a solution in and of themselves. Anxiety has real physiological and psychological effects. Minimizing them only makes people feel more isolated. Negating the reality of an emotion/experience that is tearing someone apart inside doesn't help, especially if they don't understand what it is they're feeling.

But…how do you get the physical sensation to blend with the emotion? How do I manage to connect them, fuse them together in my consciousness when they appear to be wired separately in my psyche?

It's hard to convey instructions with words, when what you're trying to describe is an emotion connected to a physical sensation. This is difficult for so many people. Let's begin the process with Questions:

Ask:

- What am I feeling physically?
- What am I feeling emotionally?
- When am I feeling these things?
- Do I understand what started this rise in anxiety?
- What exactly was the catalyst?

The following three steps are an excellent place to begin *your* journey into self-awareness and personal progress.

NA: Take Time for Self-Reflection—What else is going on at that time every day? Why do I feel this way at 3 o'clock? What is creating this 'jittery,' 'unsettled' sensation? Oh! That's why! (When you pinpoint what the repeated problem is.) Now *that* makes sense.

HER: Using a journal to track patterns between physical feelings and emotional states can really enhance your journey through mindfulness and self-reflection exercises. Over time there is often a pattern that emerges. Tracking those moments of physical sensations and using those statistics to see how they correspond to your emotional state may help you be better equipped to combine the two, currently acknowledged separate 'things,' and thus more easily identify 'a feeling.'

NAT: I needed a professional to help me put two and two together. It didn't make sense to me, and I swam in my own whirlpool of confusion far too long. I definitely appreciated the 'line' thrown to me by the therapist. Knowledge is power, and I'd learned something about myself, my body, and my emotions, that I just couldn't identify on my own.

Normal is an Illusion. What is Normal for the Spider is Chaos for the Fly.

HER: Way back in college I participated in an experiment that was supposed to help reduce and perhaps even eliminate the stress response/fear of 'something.' They asked me what I was most afraid of. I told them, spiders. A young student running the 'labs' came by for four weeks, with a jar of spiders. He told me they were completely harmless. He held the jar and then asked me to hold the jar. Okay. First goal accomplished. It was still 'icky' but I was okay. The next step involved getting the little spider out of the jar and letting it crawl on my hand. This was so much more difficult. I hated it, but to help with the

goal of the experiment, I allowed it. The fourth week, I opened the jar, got out the spider, and sat there while it crawled on my hand and wrist. The young man was thrilled. He took notes, saying how amazing it was that by confronting this phobia we had shown that we could 'desensitize my fear' to the aforementioned spider. After penning all of that, he looked up and saw my silent tears making a slow journey down my cheek. He asked, "This hasn't been successful at all, has it?"
"Uhm, no, not so much."

First, you need to recognize your trigger and your increasing distress. Identify it thoroughly. Second, develop a plan for what you're going to do when you're exposed to the source of your distress.

What is *my* plan for when I see spiders? There are three possible scenarios:

- Scream and run to get help
- Leave it alone in the corner and name it Sid
- Smash the creature to death, with prejudice

Interestingly, I usually try to find someone else to dispose of the creature. However, if one of my children is in 'danger' because of the little arachnid, I become a warrior princess, armed and ready to go to war. And yes, I have done all of those.

NAT: When the anxiety adds up and up and up, I know I'm a ticking time bomb. What do I do to survive? And what tools can I use now to build on that success?

- First, I looked for support. I had to get away from my stressor (trigger/tension/trauma/worry/person)
- Second, I had to give myself time to do quality things. This can add up to a lot of time to 're-set'

- Third, I made new friends
- Fourth, I took time to just 'be me'
- Fifth, I got a job at a peaceful day spa

HIM: Anxiety is always there. Just about everything exacerbates it. One of the worst occurrences is during what people call 'simple social interaction.' The real problem here is that there is *no map* or set of directions with which to navigate a conversation safely.

The use of scripted plans for conversations, or pre-rehearsed ideas for small talk often run in the mind of an autistic person struggling to make sense of conversations <u>*before*</u> they happen. It's exhausting, and we haven't even left home yet.

Does this feel familiar? Do you leave the house worried about the things you may need to say, but feel you never know what to say? Do you always seem to wind up in arguments with people? Do you find yourself in disagreements when it was never your intention? I'll bet you don't even know how you got there. And I mean to the point where they'll say, "I don't want to argue with you, I don't wanna have this disagreement!" And I'll respond, "I didn't know we were having an argument." Now, everyone's confused.

The previous point isn't one of my issues so much, *but* the next is. I have a never-ending running script in my mind *after* an event. Could I have done it better? I should have said… I wish I'd said…

This causes me distress without end. And to top it off, I seem to remember only bits of a conversation, not the whole thing. Sometimes I remember only a vague idea of what was said, yet rarely particulars. This causes extreme challenges within my relationships.

HER: James, Ben and I once traveled to Cedar City to participate in our granddaughter's baptismal festivities. It was during the potluck lunch and the impromptu water fight afterwards that James asked me quietly, "Hey, Diana, am I doing okay?" I knew immediately what he meant, and I was the only one there who knew how to answer the true intent of that question. To translate, 'Hey, Diana, I feel like I'm behaving okay, and I've interacted with all the grandchildren, and our new son-in-law too. I'm feeling boisterous and happy just now, BUT is my behavior socially acceptable?' The answer was a resounding, "*Yes*, James, no worries at all." And yet I could tell there had been many moments of personal concern on his part as his anxiety was ever-present.

NA: I taught my nine-year-old daughter how to self-regulate when she is overwhelmed with situations she cannot control. This is a modified 'square breathing' technique. When she feels panic beginning to build, she has learned to take in a deep breath, hold it to the count of four, and then exhale to the count of four. She has in turn taught her little sisters the same skill set when they are distraught. It is a thing of beauty.

INSIGHT 1: There are many ways to combat anxiety. Our favorite is through the power of music. James will put on a pair of earphones and focus on the beat, or listen intently for the sound of a trumpet, or the drums. This helps him block out the world. He uses this 'mind-music' melding technique anytime the world becomes too loud.

INSIGHT 2: One young granddaughter puts on instrumental music and begins to dance, often with her eyes closed. Recently, she began her 'program' but added a slightly deflated helium-filled balloon to be part of her routine while she moved to the music. Gently tapping it to stay afloat, in beat to the music, was her own invention to help process her joy (and her excess energy within the AuDHD diagnosis). This was new, since she usually just hops up and down, up and down, getting from one place to another. I love watching her creativity bring her inner self-expression to life. It's truly beautiful.

INSIGHT 3: Another tool is patience within the context of the conversation, allowing yourself to take a breath before you respond to something that was confusing and potentially hurtful. One daughter recently stated, "I'm so glad I waited for the full explanation *before* allowing my anxiety to take over and run rampant."

INSIGHT 4: Another tool that may be useful during social situations would be to have an 'exit strategy.' Having a plan to gracefully leave a conversation or environment that becomes overwhelming can provide a sense of security. Using a phrase like, 'I need to step out for a moment,' is a very polite way to let your hostess know you won't be around for a bit. Or perhaps a pre-designated quiet space in which to retreat can make these potential social hazards feel less intimidating.

5 Sensory Sensitivities/Overload

CHALLENGE: Specific sensory sensitivities, whether its lights, sounds, aromas, social chaos, etc., can make social situations overwhelming and/or uncomfortable. This may lead persons with autism to avoid social gatherings where these sensitivities are heightened. It may also create an embarrassing situation where they completely meltdown, blowup and behave poorly. Sometimes it's like watching themselves lose their self-control, knowing there is no way to stop the disaster from destroying everything in sight.

HER: So many of the things that rarely bother me are nerve-wracking to *him*. Comparison: I get overloaded when I've reached 'weary' which is way, way past tired. My patience becomes non-existent because I need to simply put myself in bed and go to sleep, in a much needed 'time-out.' The problem has been not understanding/comprehending/empathizing why *I* can re-set over night, and it can take *him* days and weeks, and then he can only handle it (life) a few hours more before he needs another lengthy re-set. *So unfair!* Yes, be prepped for that.

NOISES, in general. Do noises seem louder or more intense to your nervous system *when you are stressed?* What wouldn't normally bother you is *suddenly painful?* "Say what?" I asked. "Why are you bothered by that right now? It's never bothered you before?" (Can you sense the tension building?)

These kinds of neural sensitivities definitely occur when someone is over-stimulated, stressed, or agitated. They can occur with a migraine, post-traumatic stress, or simply from too much noise exposure. Be aware, what isn't a stressful noise to you can completely wipe out your significant other.

Loud Noises – Potential Solution: Can you handle wearing legit noise-canceling headphones or earbuds? This works for both neurotypical and divergent. This may protect you from some sensory overload. There are several different brands and designs, thankfully. James cannot tolerate the 'in the ear' device.

HER: I didn't realize this was a 'thing' for a long time. It just seemed too 'convenient' when there was still so much to get done. Why is he always leaving to his shop just as the girls get home in the afternoon? But he knew. He knew ahead of time that it was a situation he couldn't endure. And even though he couldn't explain it at the time, he knew he needed his sanctuary. The children were welcome in his shop, as long as he could keep his hands busy while they prattled on. And the overwhelm was real, tangible almost, and caused great distress.

HIM: Anytime you're not in control creates a situation fraught with potential overload. For the neurodivergent, that means every time we go out the front door.

Much of the noise in my life during these two decades came from my seven daughters, and their incessant chatter. I found it difficult to stay at the dinner table because they talked about things that simply weren't relevant to me… I found it repetitive, boring, unnecessary prattle. There didn't seem to be any real point to it. I didn't want to sit in a room while they talked about boys, make-up, dating, the cuteness of, the rudeness of, the hope, the depression, the excitement, the disappointment, (which for teenaged girls seemed to happen in twelve second cycles), what dresses to wear, what fabric to make something with, the church activities, etc. It all just sounded like irritating static and tended to drive me from the room.

HER: So much of what he described above about teenaged girls driving him away are the exact things I hold dear in my memory of that time. Their laughter, their joy, their discoveries of their talents, likes and dislikes. Their efforts to learn something new. I still cherish the happy noise of that time. I asked the girls what their favorite memories of those times were.

- All of us reading our own books, but all together in the living room
- All of us working on our own crocheting projects together

- When we sat in a circle and were able to take care of the sister's hair sitting in front of us
- Filming an historical skit together and laughing at the finished result

I feel sad for him, I really do, and everything he missed out on because his senses were overwhelmed by their noise and energy.

INSIGHT: Please don't underestimate the reality of sensory overload. When someone is overwhelmed by excessive sensory input—whether from bright lights, strong smells, loud noises, or an overload of social interaction—their ability to process information and respond rationally diminishes drastically. In those moments, they are not simply being dramatic or difficult; their nervous system is genuinely in distress.

Approach this challenge with as much patience and understanding as possible. Remember that the person experiencing overload is no longer in full control of their reactions. Their brain is doing its best to cope, but the flood of sensory input can make logical thinking, clear communication and self-regulation nearly impossible. Instead of pushing for immediate engagement or expecting them to 'snap out of it,' offer a calm, reassuring presence. Creating a quiet, low-stimulation space, if possible, and allowing them the time they need to recover, along with your patience and support, can make all the difference.

Special Interests

CHALLENGE: Autistic individuals often have intense interests in specific topics. While these interests can be a source of joy and fulfillment, they may also limit opportunities for social interaction if others don't share the same interests. Additionally, this tends to limit the capacity for meaningful employment that makes enough money to support a family as well.

Many autistic people have highly focused interests, often from a very young age. For younger children it can be dinosaurs, a certain cartoon character, or a train like Thomas the Tank Engine. Older children need to be exposed to various hobbies as they grow so that they may step into a new focus, perhaps in a similar occupation. My mother called it 'expanding your horizons.' They may discover they love art, music, gardening, animals, cars, or math and numbers, as well as the topics they fell in love with as toddlers.

HER: I remember Ben playing in his favorite spot in the sandbox, creating a 'road' around himself and lining up the cars in very specific order. It had to be exactly right, extremely precise. Ben's play offers a glimpse into some of the ways autism works in relation to routines, patterns, and sensory experiences.

His preference for that specific spot so early in life showed me his strong attachment to familiar environments. In a world that often felt overwhelming, he had a designated space of security and predictability. As is common among autistic individuals, lining up his cars in a specific order brought out his need for structure and control. His mind created order and he found comfort in patterns and repetition.

As I reflect back on this memory of his play, I wonder if it may also have served a sensory purpose. The feel of the sand, the visual alignment of the cars, and the structured, predictable process of arranging them gave him a sense of peace. For many autistic individuals, these forays into their preferred repetitive activities helps them manage sensory input and maintain emotional balance. Why can I say this? I observed his play and how it affected him, even before I knew he was autistic.

Ben's sandbox play was more than just play—I see it now as an expression of how his mind engages with the world. Through that play in the past, and his other activities now, he finds order, focus and even a form of self-regulation in a world that often confuses and overwhelms him.

I understand so much more about James now too, since analyzing our son. On one hand James' focus on trains brings joy to the family. He has built several large-scale train cars that the grandchildren have been thrilled to help him 'test' to see if they work on the rails. On the other hand, days can go by when we never see James because his mind is fully consumed with his craft. All he seems to need is the shop and the tools, and his complete satisfaction found in the work of creation.

INSIGHT: Please, please, validate the need for exploration of a focused interest, or its nearest similar skill. These are the things they will excel in, because they find meaning in the pursuit of their interests.

Meaning, value, job satisfaction. For most of us, these are the things that drive us, motivate and inspire us to do the things we do on a daily basis. I have been 'pleased, satisfied, fulfilled' many times as I work to reach goals and achieve dreams. He has rarely-to-never experienced job satisfaction. What?! How is that possible? You housed the family, put food on the table and spent hours in your shop. What would 'satisfaction' feel like, to you? The majority of the time, he can't find the words to answer that question.

I admit the level of frustration created by this dynamic within the scope of our marriage has been significant. For him, the rest of the world rarely even exists. For me, I have a score of things to do, to think about, and goals to accomplish for the future.

For many on the spectrum, there is no such thing as 'the future.' James told me several times as we discussed one of our daughters, 'Diana, she is like a wolf. There is no past, there is no future. She lives in the 'now.' She wants to eat when she feels hungry and sleep when she is tired. She likes to play when she is happy.' I am able to understand this in a cerebral way. My emotions have trouble with it though, because the future is so tangible to me, and I work diligently to prepare for many possible outcomes. So, living in the now, living only for today, really, really bugs me.

HER NOTE TO THE WORLD: There will need to be a much more in-depth discussion on this topic, in another platform. Those who've been diagnosed much later in life often have honed skills in their area of focus. It would be most helpful for the ND to be sought out and allowed to share their skills. Identifying and incorporating their wide variety of creativity would be an enormous boon to society.

For example, James is a master model maker, with extensive skill in prototyping and silicone rubber mold making. I believe his life would have been much more fulfilled had we understood the specific needs that are so prevalent in the autistic community. I believe a city with a *Why Things Work The Way They Do* interactive museum would have been an excellent place to pass on the skills to a rising generation, via classes and the running of train tracks, cars, launching rockets, etc. How to measure, build, create, and find joy in understanding scientific things. With someone else in charge (of course), James could build anything needed for various areas of this facility. I believe it could be epic!

The need to support a family, and spending decades in multiple jobs that caused severe trauma, and thus contributed to depression and mental health issues, did not serve him well. And yes, it was traumatic for this caregiver too. I had *so* much on my plate as we figured things out over decades. Frankly, that was too long, and wasted *so* much potential joy, leaving us both with feelings of distress and despair instead.

We are again at the beginning of a worker's cycle. Ben wanted to be a blacksmith. The closest skill I could find to that was becoming a welder. Ben now has a certificate. However, as with many of the neurodivergent, he doesn't have a standard twenty-four-hour circadian sleep rhythm. He often cannot sleep consistently, so how does he hold down a job consistently every day? His teachers do not believe he will ever hold down a standard job. If that is the case, and so far rings true, how do I help him use this skill so he finds emotional fulfillment in welding creativity? (I know, I'm talking from an NT point of view right now, but I'm hoping he could. He seems to be content simply sitting at the computer playing games right now, yet I feel he's capable of so much more than that.)

Can you imagine the worker morale and daily satisfaction these individuals would have if they could use their skill set to benefit a community in a truly meaningful way? It would be outstanding and might encourage hope, better mental health and self-worth. I believe as a society and as neighbors, we can all do better.

7 Difficulty Understanding Social Norms

CHALLENGE: Autistic individuals may find it difficult to understand social norms and expectations, which can lead to misunderstandings or social faux pas. This can make it harder for them to connect with others and build friendships.

HER: One day, early in our marriage, I was hungry and decided after I ate that I would bring James a snack plate.

"Why are you doing this?" he asked.

"What do you mean? I had a snack, and I brought one to

you because I thought you might be hungry too. It's what a wife does for her spouse."

"This has never happened to me before."

"You've never had anyone bring you a snack plate?"

"No, I don't get it."

"Hon, this is part of what *love looks* like…"

INSIGHT: I laugh as I type this. 'Yes! He *can* be taught.' Over time, yes, more than two *decades* now, James learned that doing little things for someone else was a great way to 'connect.' Most of that time, he was clueless and didn't 'get it.' With his huge social disconnect and inability to read body language in *any* way, it is no wonder that he simply didn't 'note' or recognize that simple service *is* a love language. It's been more than twenty-four years now, and I celebrate the moments he brings me a glass of water, by saying, "Thank You!" and giving him a hug. This isn't the way I thought it was going to be. It's not where I'd like it to be after 'all this time' but it *is* forward progress. Thank goodness I didn't expect it to be 'fixed' right away.

HER: I say that I didn't expect things to be 'fixed' right away. And yet, realistically, there are many days my heart breaks as I feel unnoticed, unappreciated, and unloved. Yes, that is also a truthful, hard dynamic in this relationship. I remember spending one particular day running all over, getting children registered for school, finishing up summer harp lessons, doing laundry, asking kids to fold the laundry while I took another child to town for immunizations, etc. It was a long day. After dinner, while helping Ro sign the last of her registration papers for high school, she realized the date she was writing. She looked up and said, "Mom, wasn't today your birthday?" This became one of my less awesome parent moments as I growled at the group of girls in the kitchen and ranted for a moment about how, yes, it was my birthday, but had any one of them (there were five teenaged daughters living at home at this time) bothered to fold laundry or do the dishes I'd asked for help with as I drove them around, orchestrating their lives to flow perfectly, being ignored and taken completely for granted? I was feeling really low by the end of that day. And then, James came home and pulled into the driveway. He excitedly called out, "Diana! Come on out, okay?" I did, just as he was opening the van's rear door.

"Look! See what I got. You've been wanting us to start a fence over in that corner," (pointing south and west) "so I decided to get the poles and a few crossbars today."

"Oh. Why?"

"Well, because I think it's time to do that project."

"Oh. No other reason? Just because?"

"Well, yes, it seemed like a good idea…"

"Okay. Uhm, and not because you know it's my birthday?"

"Uhm, no, is that today?"

Sigh.

During this time frame, however, I had a dear friend who told me I was looking at everything through the wrong lenses. She recognized how I put my whole soul into my family, and how much joy I found in this love language. I'm so grateful she also saw a bad habit I had and was brave enough to call me on it. Reggie asked, "Why would you deliberately set yourself up for disappointment year after year? Do you *want* to feel hurt and unhappy?" The simple answer was, "No, of course not!"

Isn't it interesting how 'stuck' you can be and not even realize you can create a completely new paradigm, choosing a different path with intent? Who knew? I was so overwhelmed with nine children, and James, that I couldn't see this option.

James *never* remembers his *own* birthday, let alone anyone else's. Reggie told me I would have a much happier life if I took matters into my own hands, decided where I'd really like to go out to dinner, make the reservations, and tell James we were going out on, say, Friday night, to celebrate my birthday. This way I get to dress up, put on make-up, and eat something I actually like. James was warned that we were going out in advance, and this way his personal schedule could make room for an outing for the two of us.

Huge amounts of, "Duh! Diana!" Right? Mostly 'yes,' and a little 'no.' It took time and forgiveness on my part to learn how to properly work things out with an autistic man. And then there was the matter of my traitorous heart. I craved my happily-ever-after marriage, and I was *never* going to have the life/marriage/relationship I had envisioned. Being able to accept, forgive, and adjust is hard, painstaking work. That adjustment was truly one of the most difficult things. To be completely honest, it still is from time to time.

I had to learn and accept that what I had dreamed of (and thought I was living) was dead. It was an impossible thing and would never arrive. No matter what, it cannot be real because your spouse isn't wired in the neurotypical way. Romance isn't going to be a 'thing' in your life, because he doesn't really comprehend what that means, and definitely doesn't know how to create that kind of a moment. Sometimes, just 'basic thoughtfulness' won't happen either.

I was living in a very real, tangible mental space, yet it took a *long* time for me to realize that this 'reality' was actually my own mental myth. My thoughts and dreams about marriage, my beliefs and assumptions all rolled up into that concept which made up the paradigm I was invested in. It took my loving neighbor's question, "Why would you deliberately set yourself up for disappointment year after year? Do you *want* to feel hurt and unhappy?" to set me straight. I had two choices. Choose to do things differently, with the intent of dealing with things as they really were to maximize happiness within these newly understood boundaries; or… leave this situation to create a life more in line with my current mental paradigm.

How hard is it to change your personal paradigm? What are the difficulties involved in a paradigm shift?

I cannot answer the depth these questions require here, however, this much I can say. I began to seriously question my relationship, and what I was doing. Why would I choose to stay in a relationship that hurt so much? On the one hand, he was such an a**. Yep, not gonna down-play that one. However, I can admit that this assessment is viewed through my NT perspective. He has a completely different thought-process, beliefs, assumptions, etc. all rolled up into his ND paradigm. Frankly, the two of them are incommensurable (love this word!) What does this mean? It means that these two things cannot be judged by the same standard since they have no common standard of measurement. Whoa! It gets deep here. You doing okay?

Let's try this one. Certain qualities which lack a basis for comparison are therefore not comparable in any meaningful way. I believe I know what true love and commitment could look like in a wonderful relationship. He doesn't have a clue about love, or about the realities of commitment. And that's only *one* paradigm between those in an NT and ND relationship. Each one will look a little different. This one, is ours.

I thought about leaving this relationship and did a couple times. In the long run though, for me personally, it boiled down to this thought process. When you have a little baby boy, and after several years you discover he's autistic, do you get rid of him? My answer was, and is, "No!" You teach him, train him, and hope he becomes a viable, useful and productive member of society.

Now, take that same process. You marry a man that you do not know is autistic. Your marriage isn't easy, often seriously rocky, yet you hope you will both grow into it. Then, you both discover that he is autistic, and *that's* why certain things are the way they are in your relationship. You love him. You married him. But now that there is a diagnosis in place, and *so* much begins to make sense—do you get rid of him? Most of what is hard isn't going to change. You know that now. This is going to keep being hard. Harder than anything you may ever have dreamed of. So, do you just let him go?

I'll admit it, I didn't want to, *and* I wanted to. There was so much pain, hurt, anguish, and sorrow in our relationship. Having tried so hard, feeling like such a failure, nothing was improving, feeling like I was missing critical need-to-know information, was much like that dreaded NOS evaluation on my girls' IEP in school. I didn't know where to even begin. Could our situation improve? I just didn't know anymore.

FINAL INSIGHT: Focus on the positives in your social interaction. Do you love the same music? That's a win. Do you have moments of joy as you dance together (or with grandkids) to some awesome music in the kitchen? Another win. Do you enjoy the time he shares his talents with you (before he monologues)? Do you enjoy taking a walk together in the evening? Have you built something you want to keep? If the answer is yes, for both of you, then focus on those things to create your own, specially designed one-of-a-kind partnership.

8 | Emotional vs Emotionless

CHALLENGE: People with autism *can* experience and feel emotions. However, they may express them differently than others. For example, if they need time to process their emotions, they may appear emotionless or expressionless. Those without autism often assume you're not affected by a situation because they don't see you expressing emotion.

HIM: I don't have a passion for most anything, except creative building. I'm not a touchy-feely entity. I don't easily register emotions of any kind on my face but that doesn't mean I'm emotionless. I don't think I'll ever 'express feelings' the way an NT person does.

    a. There is an aversion to physical contact or other more intimate gestures.

        i. For example: hugging, touching, kissing people when you meet them. It's not that I don't want to do it, it just doesn't occur to me that there's a 'right' thing to do when shaking hands, pats on the back, etc.

        ii. Yes, this means all people, including my wife. I love her. I love our physical connection, but I don't always want to hold hands or hug or kiss her goodbye—or hello, for that matter, or any of these kinds of things.

    b. I'm not sure what's socially appropriate in most situations, and I may not be comfortable doing, even if I did know. It is *okay* to not be a touchy-feely person.

    c. Do Not coach me to do this. I'm an adult, I'll do it if I choose to, or not.

    d. It's important to share how you feel about it. Otherwise, how would anyone know? It is okay to let them know. Let's please be clear, up front, and *kind*.

    e. Formerly, I believed 'any sort of disagreement, argument, or emotional chaos is to be avoided at almost any cost. No price is too high to make it end.'

i. Unfortunately, this mechanism caused the most harm in my relationships. There *is* a price too high and forgetting where to draw the line is an enormous mistake.

I own a coffee mug with a comment on it that is *very* me. It sports the purple Minion from Despicable Me 2 and it reads, 'Be yourself. People don't have to like you, and you don't have to care.' I have spent too many years worrying about what others think about me, my behavior, my lack of appropriate humor and social skills. My life has felt like a nightmare. But this minion made me rethink that, and I'm learning to be at peace with myself.

HER: While I believe the above meme has a needed space in his life, I have often felt stuck at the end of his 'I don't care.' It feels like he's more of an emotional brick wall. My range of emotion is much larger, and his is so much smaller to the point of feeling that he doesn't have an emotional range at all. This is not accurate; it is simply how I feel sometimes. He has mentioned he believes his mother was overly emotional and he has had a great deal of difficulty deciphering if his behaviors, reactions, etc. were what they should have been. With this late-diagnosis, James has begun to reevaluate past events.

As we learned about our son, Ben, we learned about ourselves. Ben simply cannot relate to that wider range of emotion. Sometimes he tells me he simply doesn't have the words to express stuff. He'll stand there with his mouth opening to say something, and then closing it with nothing making it through, repeatedly. This frustrates him so much.

HIM: Everybody walks through a minefield in their life, but neurotypicals seem to see the mines and skillfully avoid many of them. This neurodivergent individual does not, especially where emotions are concerned. Diana has explained that there are tasteful and appropriate moments for affection — timing matters. That part often escapes me. I don't often understand boundaries.

HER: His inability to pick up on my nonverbal cues, or even understand my explicit verbal instruction, leads him to complete misunderstanding of my motives, or reasoning behind my social discomfort when he behaves in certain ways. He doesn't comprehend why he's so far in left field he may as well be in another country. Additionally, when he is trying to make sense of what confused him in the first place, he tends to put things together negatively; she meant to hurt me, insult me, or she's condemning me. My intent in explaining was not to be hurtful at all but to help him learn more about what makes me tick. *Right there, we both need to pause, breathe, and ask,* "I don't think I understood, can we clarify what you were asking, or what you heard?"

JEN: Be brave enough to create change by looking within and working to become your best self. When positive change begins with you, a spouse will often look up and join you. I may not be as in touch with my emotions/feelings (being autistic) or be able to define them easily, but I *have* them. Don't let your spouse/partner dictate who you are, what you say, or how you feel. Own yourself. Love yourself. Create yourself.

INSIGHT 1: Many with autism struggle to put feelings together with their attendant physical sensations. There are multitudes of images online describing emotions and the nuanced variables that are associated with it. For instance, 'joy' has many relatives. Feel free to meet 'happy,' 'pleased,' and 'thrilled' as well, and yet each is different.

INSIGHT 2: Sometimes we get trapped in our emotions and habits. Sometimes our style of communication is all wrong. However, if you're advised that you just need to communicate more, and you're using the wrong type of destructive communication, it will actually make things worse. If your cycle includes blaming each other while defending yourself, you're spiraling down a whirlpool of hurt-blame-pain-sorrow-distress that is difficult to stop. It's too hard to see your part in it because you're too focused on the other person's negative qualities. "Well, if they would just…everything would be fine."

At this point, the problem isn't communication. The problem is safety, comprehension and compassion. There is a space for healthy, productive conflict. If you no longer open up to each other or allow yourself to be vulnerable like when you were dating, you're at risk. The couples that stay together will learn to listen, being curious and respectful. These couples will say 'I'm sorry' more, with sincerity. These are couples that can break free of disastrous, toxic and lethal communication cycles. It's okay to try new ways of interacting with one another, especially if the goal is to enhance and improve your marriage/partnership.

INSIGHT 3: A theme is developing as this book is being written. Breathe. Patience. Love. Forgiveness. Charity. These things are required in full measure as you deal with any relationship. The recipe here, though, is a double portion shaken together.

9 There Are No Words For Emotions – Alexithymia

CHALLENGE: Can you imagine living with less than 70% of the communication clues available to you, in a world that believes if you can speak, you probably understand? The toll it would take; not understanding, comprehending, or worse, completely misunderstanding—and then not having the ability to describe it so you can be understood? This is a definition for a nightmare. It's like trying to complete a crossword puzzle with only thirty letters, but there are one hundred spaces.

Individuals with autism are known to experience this difficulty not only with communication, but also the understanding of their own emotions, non-verbal expression of emotion, and last but not least, being able to interpret others' emotions from facial expressions and body language.

This challenge has a specific name. What is Alexithymia, exactly? It is when you have no words to describe how you're feeling. It could also be stated as those having difficulties understanding their own emotions, and/or describing them.

HER: James still has virtually no understanding of emotions or feelings and what they mean, how to describe them, or how to express them. There is a serious disconnect. (Diana, I don't know what love is…)

Nat finds it so hard to teach her children to use emotional words with more depth. She asks one, "If Kian took *your* toy, how would *you* feel?" They usually respond with, "I'd be so mad!" Then she tells me, "Mom, I'm trying to help them branch out and describe the problem. I can't get them to use other words to verbalize 'mad.' It is *so* frustrating."

INSIGHT: There are ways to alleviate parts of this problem, one point at a time. There are many free downloads online for teaching children about their emotions. There are many essential oils that can assist in emotional regulation practices as well.

When it comes to someone diagnosed much later in life, the simple downloads may be far beneath them, having figured out the basic emotions already. James found that writing a book, *A*

Home Among the Stars: Trials of the Elected, helped him think about things from a different perspective, enabling him to give his characters basic emotions. However, he still doesn't know how to describe more nuanced feelings and definitely cannot quantify his own.

Time and effort will be your friends in this realm. I would suggest making it relevant to the person. I know, that seems so obvious, right? However, for example, James loves the Minions. We found a chart that had these characters with various facial emotions and attendant feelings defined and hung it on our wall for a time. This proved useful.

Get creative, let your imagination have wings. This is part of creating a joyful journey. It's hard! I know how hard it is. 'Choose with intention, keep moving forward.'

10 Bullying and Social Exclusion

CHALLENGE: We need friends, desperately. Unfortunately, autistic individuals may be more vulnerable to bullying due to their differences in social behavior. Autism can often create the appearance of being weak, either mentally or physically because a person doesn't know how to deal with stressful situations, doesn't have the capacity for the quick quip or response, and thus become easy targets.

NA: My little Mel is eight. She is mercilessly bullied from the moment she leaves our home, until she gets off the bus and runs into my arms afterwards. Just the other day a problem arose as she was telling her friends her opinion on long-distance friendships. She has a friend she dearly misses who lives far away. Because she shared her emotions, they began to call her a variety of names, which she did not understand. Her anxiety levels were extremely high when she arrived home and as she related the story, I had to explain terms that were beyond her years, and although it helped Mel begin to understand, she now has heightened anxieties. She no longer wants to attend any events of any kind. Her tender soul is in anguish, and she is now thoroughly self-conscious and even more vulnerable. We continue working with counselors and teachers to counter these issues, but we don't see how this can be repaired when the daily abuse just keeps mounting. She is using the following tools at this time: Square breathing, remembering who loves her, essential oils, and her own personal positivity mantra. When her emotions are high, it is harder for her to access these tools on her own, but she is doing better, especially with her breathing.

HIM: Most of the bullying I endured was in high school. I remember a series of incidents specifically designed to create a no-win situation. I was a very light-weight young man, zero bulk and mostly bones. I would be backed into a wall by two bigger boys and one would accuse me of calling the other boy 'something.'

I responded, "No I didn't!"

And the second boy would say, "Are you calling me a liar?"

And I had two options at that point, to either not say anything at all which would probably have been the wisest, or to say, 'I'm not calling you a liar…'

To which I was pressed, 'So you did call me that!' And I was trapped. At that point, my distress caused tears to start streaming down my face. That had been the goal, and they would walk off, laughing.

I wanted to play in sports because I hoped maybe I would look a little more interesting to girls. I tried out for Junior Varsity Football and made the team. Immediately a problem surfaced. I simply couldn't remember the plays. I didn't lose interest, but I did quit the team. It was a way to save my pride so I was no longer humiliated when I didn't meet expectations.

I tried out for basketball too. I didn't make the team because I couldn't dribble very well. I could make some shots, but the coordination for everything else was suspect. They kept me on as 'manager,' which meant I was the towel and water boy.

I couldn't talk to girls. I had normal teenage dreams and desires but had *no* idea how to engage in conversation. I was so insecure. I used to go to dances put on by my local church. I would ask a girl to dance, and if she said yes, I would stay, because the ice had been broken, and my courage boosted. But if the first girl I asked said no, I would go home.

Feel good moment: I did letter in track while in high school. Some things in life take perseverance, and I found one thing I could do, and I stuck to it for four years. I did the hurdles and the triple jump, and I ran the middle distance in the 440. I didn't do anything spectacular those years, I simply kept trying.

INSIGHTS: Find a friend who truly understands and supports you—a 'safe person' or 'navigator' with whom you can be yourself without fear of judgment. It's okay to ask for help when you need it; you don't have to figure everything out on your own.

For those who are neurotypical, make the effort to look beyond your usual social circles and extend genuine friendship to someone who may struggle to reach out. Be the person who offers understanding, patience, and inclusion. A little effort can make a world of difference.

Connection matters, and there is strength in coming together. Everyone deserves a place where they feel valued and supported.

11 Difficulty with Empathy and Perspective-Taking

CHALLENGE: Some autistic individuals may find it difficult to understand others' perspectives and feelings, which can impact their ability to build and maintain meaningful relationships.

Mel: "Mom! Miri threw this at me! I don't like it when she throws things at me!"

NA: "Now Miri, think about it. Would you like it if Mel threw something at you? No?" *pauses for Miri to speak.* "Yes, it would probably hurt. Would you want her to do that? No? Well, then? What needs to happen now?"

Miri: "I will apologize, Mama."

NA: "That's my girl!"

A short time later…

Miri: "Mom! Mel threw this back at me! I'm so mad. Why did she do that?"

Mel: "Because you threw it at me first!"

NA: "But Mel, she apologized and said she wouldn't do it again."

Miri: "I guess I can throw whatever I want, whenever I want, because it doesn't matter, right?"

NA: "Oh, my ever-lovin' stars!"

It has been claimed by several online sources that autistic people are more likely to be single than those who are neurotypical. One of the reasons was demonstrated in Ben's 4th grade counseling session.

HER: The counselors were teaching him the difference between 'flexible brains' and 'rigid brains.' He didn't care for the exercise especially since I was advised to keep using the same vocabulary at home to help him remember it. When I asked him a question about the idea of 'flexible brains,' he growled at me like a dinosaur. This response will not go over well in the future if this same visceral response comes into play anytime he hears a request he does not appreciate.

Do you, the caretaker spouse, often feel like you don't get the support you need in life? Do you feel your partner doesn't recognize when you're sick or when you might need help with the house or the kids?

This is when you might feel he's completely unresponsive to the things you need from a partner. I would posit he's simply unaware. Yes, I mean that. We might think he 'should' be able to see it, but I can tell you from experience that he does *not* and is oblivious. Reciprocity is not a 'thing,' it doesn't exist, and they're not wired for it.

He truly doesn't understand there are basic needs for love, affection, and attention. These things are often not understood and so he doesn't ever follow through, and you're left feeling that he doesn't care.

I've gone way down *that* rabbit hole, feeling so abandoned. How could I have ever fallen for this self-centered, selfish, unfeeling, narcissistic...? Yeah, this is a bad space. Breathe, dear one, calm!

If you've discovered that the inability to describe or relate emotions is something you or your friend/partner/spouse struggles with, here are a few items that may help you navigate your relationship:

- Try to be as direct as you can when communicating
- Give them space when they ask for it (especially after they have been overstimulated)

- — Be understanding if they need a break from social gatherings
- Try not to introduce too much change all at once
- Be mindful that some things will be easier for you to do than for your partner
  - — Adjust accordingly (e.g., household chore split, who handles the minutiae of paperwork better, laundry, sweeping, fire starting, chopping wood, etc.)
- Be respectful of the need for structure and routine.

Beginning and maintaining relationships with an autistic person can be wonderful, but there is an enormous learning curve as well. This curve exists simply because, as a typical, I feel I must learn and be aware of so much more.

- One of the largest adjustments is finding the patience needed to explain social cues and norms, repeatedly.
- In spite of this huge dilemma, we can learn to safely navigate the ocean of feelings and learn to describe what we're feeling, together. I think this goes for both diverse and typically wired folks.
- Often, he doesn't have feelings. He feels disconnected and numb. When he does have feelings, it becomes complicated by having no words to describe his feelings (alexithymia).

In a nutshell, autistic people are more than capable of love, learning how to communicate it, and remaining in romantic relationships.

HER: How can you tell if an autistic person loves you? Especially if they don't understand what love is, or 'should look like?' I was told by a counselor that a ND person is showing love when they open up their world to you, call you to come share some time with them, draw you in and share their hobbies with you. If they reach out to you in this way, seem content to simply share and 'be' with you, then they may have feelings for you.

I understand this. James, after almost twenty-five years of marriage, still has *no* idea what love is, and has told me so. I'm not telling tales out of school. He doesn't really comprehend the idea of romance, or how to create an event that would be considered romantic and struggles with the idea that there's more than one way to share affection. There are truly five love languages. He is not well-versed in any of them. I miss romance. Sometimes I'm so lonely I could just cry. The connection created by romance is definitely MIA in this relationship between **HIM** (ND) and **HER** (NT).

I have kept a journal. I share this letter with permission from **HIM**. This letter clearly shows a few interesting things. It demonstrates an inability to find words that describe emotions. It definitely shows a lack of understanding and confusion. He apologizes for being like Ben and inflicting Ben and autism into my life (which I have never once complained about). He acknowledges inappropriate social behavior; however, he doesn't apologize for his behavior in this scenario. It is rare that he does. (And that's an entirely different subject for another time.) He does, however, promise to try harder.

> Diana, I was wrong in how I handled the situation. I know this even though I cannot put into words why. Since you left to pick up Ben, I have been trying to wrap my head around it. What came to mind is what usually happens when anyone takes Ben out of his immediate situation. His demeanor plummets. He is truly my son and I apologize for whatever there is in my DNA that inflicted that upon him and consequently you.

I will put extra effort into trying to recognize, during moments of frustration, that what peaceful demeanor I usually maintain is slipping away and to seek out your calming influence instead of withdrawing into a protective shell and hurting you.

There is another aspect that I think might contribute to why I respond to certain things in specific ways, though it will take me time to process what is in my head, because right now I doubt I could put it into words that would make sense. However, so you aren't left completely in the dark and wondering I will say this.

The last time I talked to (our daughter) I was left totally drained. She was so full of hate; all I wanted to do was find a way to hide from her. Kind of how Ben deals with uncomfortable situations. When it comes to you it's just the opposite. I do enjoy your company and calming influence. I think when I get frustrated, I don't know how to handle the situation. I'm focused on a project element and the interruption drags up the autistic response rather than a normal one.

Again, I'm still trying to process this idea.

I will make an effort to talk to you rather than hide in, I guess maybe insecurity, and talk to you.

Jamie

HER: Empathy and being able to see another's perspective will continue to be something to be worked on, talked about, and thought through. If this sounds like your journey with a late-diagnosed autistic partner, may peace be upon you. May patience be your constant companion. The only insight I can share with you is that relationships are precious things, and if both of you are 'in it to win it' together, it will help you breathe big, deep calming breaths when things get tough.

Note: I'd been with him thirteen years now. Note from journal 2013: I remember when an older woman listened to me complain about an ailment. Her response was usually, 'Oh, I've felt that way. When it happened to me, though…' and she would then tell her story that was bigger, and worse than my problem. Because I rarely felt heard, I learned to respond differently.

When *he* has a hard day, I'll look at him and say, "Oh, I'm so sorry, James." Or "That must have been rough." Or I'll hug him, which usually ends up with a neck and shoulder rub as well as I try to truly hear him. Last night I said, "Oh, it's been a long day. I've had to work really hard." And James replied, "I had to work a really long day too." I smiled at him. I said, "Now, not today, but sometime in the future, I'd like to be treated with sympathy, the way I treat you…" What I had hoped to say was that a comment, or a statement, or even just a hug with murmured understanding would be so nice. I wasn't given time to explain any of that validating type of behavior. You threw a temper tantrum instead.

INSIGHT: Just Be Aware: being in a relationship with an autistic person simply looks a lot different than you may be expecting. This is one of those times when you want to sit a moment and truly contemplate how some of these scenarios may play out in your life. You know when you look back and think: If only I had taken a moment to pause and consider before I leaped headlong into…whatever it is you wish you'd done differently? This may be one of those moments. Take time to truly think about what you're willing to sacrifice for this relationship. I believe there will be many required of you, the NT spouse. James will tell you he hasn't been required to make that many adjustments. He thinks one way, and there isn't that much that shifts him out of his pathway. He'll also tell you that I'm an incredibly balanced and even-keel person and that it's wonderful to live with someone who isn't all over the map emotionally. That's really sweet, but inaccurate.

12 | Autistic Burnout

CHALLENGE: Autistic burnout is the inevitable physical and mental exhaustion experienced by autistic persons as a result of doing everything possible to mask their differences in order to blend in.

Are you 'toast' after you come home from going places? For example; simply walking outside, going shopping, keeping appointments. These can render you completely exhausted. You did it, but the energy it took to do it, to mask yourself, to camouflage, to suppress your true self to make sure other people feel comfortable—is life-sapping.

HER: Before we knew what this was, this problem destroyed several business endeavors I had spent countless hours creating for *him*. He'd get to a certain point, kind of freak out and tell me he couldn't do it anymore, and that I was to take down the website because he was done. He wasn't going to do this anymore. At all. End of story. Finito. This nearly destroyed our marriage.

HIM: What has brought me to burnout before? Everything that isn't self-initiated. Or asking me a question and expecting an immediate answer. Basically, my understanding of life's expectations are so much bigger than my ability to meet them. I hide to get away from the overwhelm.

After an event at our home and the guests leave, that's when I crash, I'm nearly nonfunctional. I'm not just 'done,' I'm utterly worn out. There simply is nothing left for all the other activities that now need 'energy.' The train has reached the end of the line.

My family still questions why. It's because I finally got to stop, sit, rest, be myself again, and my proverbial train is able to process and unload the social baggage.

HER: Our son can take inordinate amounts of time in the bathroom. "Hey Ben, you had a shower and it's like forty-five minutes later. What did you do up there?" He just escaped the world and took his time, to unwind, to relax, to decompress, to feel free. Ultimately, Ben has *no* sense of the passing of time anyway, so for him, it doesn't register as 'too long.'

Burnout, as I've seen in several grandchildren, is meltdowns, reduction in age-appropriate behavior, as well as tummy trouble.

NA: My sweet Mel has frequent tummy problems and is always exhausted. Her preferred method of dealing with the stressors in her life is to hide under her blanket, or to quietly cuddle the kittens. Miri gets louder and louder, repeating herself until she gains your attention. By then, I'm done, What! Because she invaded my activity, and re-direction or shifting course is a difficult thing for adults too. But, I have to remember to breathe, for she is just a tiny child diagnosed with extra-large emotions. Even though it's exhausting, I'm the one who needs to show her how to regulate, ground, and adapt herself. It all starts with me breathing and not screaming, *"What!"*

Common Symptoms of Autistic Burnout for Children:

Physical Symptoms
- Chronic Weariness
- Headaches
- Sleep disturbances
- More prone to illness
- Loss of speech

Emotional Symptoms
- More frequent emotional outbursts
- Increased anxiety
- Greater irritability
- New or deeper depression

Behavioral Symptoms
- Increasing meltdowns
- Social withdrawal
- Reduced communication
- Difficulty with personal hygiene
- Loss of some motor skills
- Lack of interest
- Heightened aggression

What is it in life that brings someone to this precipice of peril?

- **Sensory Overwhelm:** the brain becomes overwhelmed by information. Places like noisy classrooms or crowded grocery stores can feel like an assault, literally
- **Social Exhaustion:** This involves pretending to be 'normal' so they fit in. It is so taxing to wear a 'social mask'
    - Forcing eye contact
    - Trying to eliminate their need for stimming or hand-flapping
    - Trying to have 'appropriate' facial expressions

Supporting Well-Being

Whether you're in the middle of a current episode, or looking for ways to avoid burnout altogether, your support will go a long way. 'You cannot pour from an empty cup' is a well-known adage. Social camouflage and the simple drain of everyday living requirements will deplete their 'cup,' while a good sleep routine, rest, and restorative activities will help fill it up.

Activities to replenish the soul:

- Art
- Play
- Creative work
- Puzzles

Possible Burnout Triggers for Adults:

Overwhelming accumulation of life stressors; a lack of support structures, meaning there is no relief from overwhelming pressures; and life expectations begin to outweigh what one feels capable of dealing with.

- Feeling devalued
- Lack of self-care
- Fear of failure
- Sensory overload
- Not knowing your limits
- Feeling misunderstood
- Too much social interaction
- Too much masking
- Being bullied, harassed
- Repeated negative experiences
- High levels of perfectionism
- Suppressing the need to stim
- Not meeting societal expectations

- Pressures of everyday life
- Trying to do more than you can manage

HIM: Autistic burnout: I had to battle that this weekend. I forced myself to watch a comedy special, so that I laughed. I wrote some, did my artwork, played my game, showered, made sure I ate. *None of these activities were required by anyone. I was able to choose for myself.* I detest expectations. Being aware of your *external* personal dialogue is challenging for any of us. Being aware of your *internal* personal dialogue takes even more consideration and effort.

HER: Your spouse (or child) is the expert of both their own body and their life. Encourage them to make their own choices about how they spend their time. Helping them become educated on what makes them 'tick,' what brings them joy and satisfaction will be critical in developing their ability to self-regulate, advocate for themselves as they mature, and maintain their mental health.

INSIGHT: Caregivers, listen up. The children won't be able to describe this to you (and many adults won't be able to either). It is up to us to keep track of the sensory triggers that have the most impact upon our loved ones. Keep a list, a journal, whatever tool works for you to monitor cause and effect. This will be important. Your knowledge will become your super power. Awareness of this mental health issue is key. It helps so much to recognize the overwhelm early and intervene before the signs become too severe and debilitating. Learn from past burnout events to understand what triggers it. The same is true for caregivers. Self-care is important to help maintain our energy levels for the demands of caring for any person round-the-clock.

This subject alone could fill another book or two.

13 Textures Are Evil

CHALLENGE: You can't tolerate certain fabrics or textures. You can become overwhelmed with an intense sense of discomfort which can quickly become agitation and anger. You have to get it off you. It's gotta come off or you're going to be over-stimulated and triggered, and you could melt down. Can you feel it? Just talking about it makes a body edgy, iffy, itchy!

HIM: Clothing. Anything that is not cotton drives me up the wall.

    a. Do you have to cut the tags off of the clothes?

        i. Frequently yes, especially if it's actually touching my skin.

        ii. I hate silk. Nylon or mesh also drives me up the wall.

    b. You simply can't wear particular clothing because it agitates you, upsets you, even though it may not really be uncomfortable. It just doesn't seem right sometimes. It could end up being anything and it simply doesn't matter, from time to time it just doesn't feel right.

HER: For some, this is a complicated yet simple issue with texture. For *him*, it is made more complex because of a skin condition known as Cholinergic urticaria. He can't stand the feel of belts, watches, hat bands, or even a ring. I've joked with the doctor that we're probably just lucky he can handle wearing clothes.

HIM: Food. The texture of food can be utterly revolting, making you physically gag. Certain smells, flavors, aromas, are completely repulsive.

- Pumpkin can make you retch; the texture is disgusting.

- Overcooked eggs! Oh, gross! The scorched, crusty film that develops when eggs sit a long time in the hot pan is just beyond my ability to—I can't even describe it. It just reeks of food in a trash can and I can't get past it.

- Even thinking of them can make you feel disgusted, or sick.

And for anyone who suffered a loss of smell during the covid pandemic and/or taste, I can tell you that when my sense of smell returned, it came back changed. I used to love the smell of peppermint essential oil. It was the number one tool we used to combat my migraine headaches. Post-covid, all peppermint smells rancid. This is extremely aggravating because I love peppermint yet cannot bear its aroma anymore.

One Solution There are so many things you can try, depending on the texture issue you deal with. Thankfully the world is filled with variety and plenty to choose from.

HER: Our son struggles to eat salads. When I asked why, he told me that it just takes too long to chew it up. He can't stand chewing that long. In this instance, to make sure he was still receiving the nutrition he needed, we developed and implemented a seven-day rotating smoothie and juicing program for him. He could drink his rainbow of salads, receive his nutrients, and remain healthy and strong.

While all of the above is real, strictly from the sensory issues prevalent with autism, for us there was an additional issue that needed to be addressed from the relationship side. One day I came home to find a letter on my desk regarding food:

> Diana, you want me to eat healthy and overall, I have no problem with that. I am however not interested in cooking on a general basis or in preparation of any

sort. If I am going to eat good then the following will have to be on hand when my system gets around to notifying me I am hungry or short of that when you do.

SALAD
1. A bag of salad fixings (Homemade or store-bought I don't care) that I can access when needed and that is not pilfered for other purposes for parts of its contents. It needs to include at least two types of lettuce and grated carrot
2. Swiss Cheese
3. Bacon (exclusive for my salads)
4. Hard Boiled Eggs (exclusive for my salads)
5. Ranch Dressing (exclusive for my salads)
6. Olives (optional)
7. Sprouts (optional)

MEAT
1. Chicken
2. Turkey
3. Hamburger

SIDE
1. Potato
2. Corn

BREAD
1. Seven or Twelve Grain bread

SOUP
1. Green Pea cooked with bacon, not ham (Must be in conjunction with one or more of the above)

CONDIMENTS

1. Dijon Mustard
2. Bullseye Barbecue sauce
3. Un-fouled butter

If the above isn't here when I want to eat then I won't likely eat anything other than what's laying around.

Sometimes he would come in to fix food while I was fixing supper. Trouble with that was, he wouldn't eat with us because he didn't like what was being fixed. He'll also fix food, sit to eat it, and never think to ask if someone else might be hungry, or peckish. When I fix food or a snack, I ask the entire home if they need something. In this instance, I let too much slide. Instead of overlooking his complete withdrawal, I wish I had been more direct and let him know that this level of isolation wasn't okay — that it was, in fact, harmful to our sense of family connection. Family dinners weren't something I felt could be optional, even in light of his autistic traits. I needed those shared meals to feel grounded and connected with everyone, and I should have communicated how important that was to me. There still needs to be some growth and development in this area of his social awareness.

INSIGHT: Smell and texture are critical for all people. Just as any person can have an aversion to cilantro because it tastes like soap (yes, this is a real thing based in DNA), an autistic person seems to have heightened issues with certain textures. This doesn't mean they're picky. It doesn't mean they're deliberately being difficult. The word we use in our home now is "discerning." It has to look right, feel right, and taste right.

14 Routine Keeps Me Grounded

CHALLENGE: Ah yes, routine – to a person with autism it can be as necessary as Wi-Fi to a teenager. Imagine you're cruising through life like a GPS: "Turn right at cereal. Proceed to four hours of hyperfocus. Slight detour into special interest. Estimated time of meltdown if plan changes: five minutes."

Routines help create order, predictability, and bring a sense of security and stability with them. Routines help us make sense of a chaotic world.

HIM: Have you ever, as a later-in-life diagnosed person, wondered why routine is so important to you, to the point of obsession? We never knew why I had such quirky needs. The diagnosis explained so much, and pieces of my personal puzzle began to fall into place.

HER: I was rearing two specific grandchildren for a number of years. Part of our evening routine, other than brushing teeth and washing little faces, was creating little singing videos together, reading scripture stories, sewing items for 18-inch dolls, or listening to Geoff Castellucci as I tucked and sang them into bed. It's amazing how much it sometimes felt like even the bedtime routine was too much when I was so busy and would sometimes skip it. I really miss it now. And I can easily understand why they would be so upset when I skipped parts. Routines created order in the lives of these little people, one with Tourette's and autism, and the other with an executive processing disorder. I'm so grateful I did as much as I did. I hope they always remember how much I love them. Sometimes, don't you just sigh over how human we are? Thankfully, these routines created very positive bonds between us.

HIM: I actually have a very specific preference for where I shop. I exclusively use a favorite grocery store, a specific hardware store, or doctor. If I go to purchase food, and they don't have the item I need, I won't generally go to another store. I'll go home and simply do without. I avoid going to another store I've never been to before. I don't know who they are or what they have or how it works. I need my store. I know where everything is, I know where to park.

I hate being interrupted once I settle on the thing I want to accomplish in my creative space. If I'm pouring resin, cutting parts, or measuring a critical space, the mental interruption disrupts the flow and it is impossible to get it back for quite some time. I find this very unsettling.

To the neuro-typical: please understand just how deeply entrenched this need is. It won't go away. It won't change. It won't be 'cured,' and it won't stop. It simply *IS*.

To the neuro-diverse: Embrace this amazing gift you have, this unique way of thinking. Help those you love understand how critically important order and routine are for your mental well-being.

HER: My daughter, Jen, prepares for trips so differently than I do. So much so that I feel like I'm traveling with Mary Poppins as we take our journey together. I love traveling with her, simply because I never know what's going to pop up out of her purse or backpack. She brings a bit of the unexpected with her, in all the right ways. She is one of the lights of my life.

And it's interesting that what seems 'a random need' from my approach to travel are very carefully thought out, organized, routinely used things she uses, and as such they aren't 'quirky' at all. They are her 'normal.' Every journey with her teaches me something new.

INSIGHT: It is well-established that routine is critically important to the autistic psyche. We won't go into the already well-documented details regarding children who are diagnosed when very young. There are many tools and recommendations for this.

15 We Don't Want to Socialize — and it's OKAY!

CHALLENGE: The idea that someone could thrive with less social interaction goes against many cultural norms about what it means to be 'connected,' 'friendly,' or 'normal.' That difference can be hard for some people to wrap their heads around. NTs often expect a back-and-forth emotional exchange. When that doesn't happen in a familiar way – like avoiding eye contact, not mirroring emotions, or keeping conversations short – it can feel like there's a wall, even when none was intended.

NT Lack of Awareness – Before learning about autism in depth, I had no idea that socializing was exhausting and distressing for those on the spectrum. Neurotypical people often see socializing as a key part of connection, friendship, and showing care. So when someone doesn't want to engage socially, it might be misread as disinterest, rudeness, or rejection – even though that's not usually the case. Many NTs are used to filling silence with small talk. NDs usually don't engage in that way and prefer quiet. It is unsettling and awkward to someone who relies on those cues. Different wiring means different needs.

HIM: I don't want to socialize. I may choose to go out with my family, but let's keep association with strangers to a minimum, if you please. Do you like to be alone when you 'should' be mingling? Is going somewhere possible only because you're with someone you know and feel comfortable with?

There *is no* moving away from my spouse at an event. If I'm by myself and trying to 'get over' the stress that says I 'should' be able to 'freely mingle.' Nope, it's impossible. It isn't going away. It hasn't changed in over sixty years, and both my wife and I learned to adjust. Admittedly, it's much easier to deal with now that we both know it is integral to my being, and not me simply being a curmudgeon.

I didn't really want to socialize even when I reached out online to mingle with singles. But after eight years as a single dad, I was very lonely in my corner of the world. Online was the only way I had to meet up with others at the time, so I made myself a profile, and waited. When Diana reached out on the same program and asked why my screen name was "Owl," it broke the ice and we began to chat. I asked her why she wanted to talk to me, and she answered that she liked a good goatee. By the time we talked on the phone, and then met in person a few months later, it was easy to talk to her. I didn't feel 'at risk' anymore.

HER: When we first got together, we used to take the kids swimming. Now, he doesn't go swimming and tells me how much he doesn't like the water. I feel like the boundaries of my cage are in diminishing mode, and I'm trapped in ever smaller spaces. This may not be accurate but it is how I feel about things just now. His continuing journey to find his best self occasionally contradicts activities we participated in before, that I thought we both enjoyed. But now he is free to tell me what he really wants, instead of pretending or 'masking' through an unwanted activity. It is a better to have this open communication. I just find it tasking when it seems to keep "shifting" and changing. This NT girl likes her routines too. The currently ever-adjusting landscape is unnerving.

My Pearl of Great Price:

There are moments in time when the stars align, and everything spins into a perfect memory. That happened back in 2006, when he was required to give the father-of-the-bride speech at his daughter's wedding reception. Was he nervous? Yes. Did he manage it perfectly? Yes.

I remember asking James if he had written down his speech. He did not 'prepare' a speech, because that made him too nervous, and he didn't feel he could do that. I had no idea what he was going to say. He didn't either, and began by thanking guests for coming. He gave a short 'warning' to her brand-new husband about the care he expected her to receive. That she was precious and had been reared with much love. James told him that she was his 'pearl of great price.' He asked him to cherish her. And then he was done.

That is a perfect memory.

HIM: I always felt like I was being insensitive, or too reclusive, or just downright ornery when an event happened. To a great extent, I never wanted to go out. I didn't really mind going bowling with my family, but going out in any way that involved close contact with strangers just sent my anxiety over-the-top. Additionally, forcing myself into a situation was even worse because my attitude would bring other people down, and *that* thought bothered me too. Sometimes, in my own skin, there simply isn't a win-win in dealing with social situations. It's just better to keep to myself.

Can you imagine never really needing to socialize? Never wanting to? Never even really thinking about it? Well, that's how it really is in our home. They rarely seek social interaction, which feels so strange. Respecting different social needs is part of understanding neurodiversity. Everyone connects in their own way.

INSIGHT: If you're neurotypical, it's important to understand that not everyone connects through social interaction. Autistic individuals may not seek out conversation, small talk, or group activities in the same way you do. It's not rejection or rudeness; it's just a different way of being. Don't take it personally. Connection doesn't always look like conversation – sometimes it's just being nearby, doing something side by side, or sharing quiet moments without pressure.

16 We Don't Understand Humor

CHALLENGE: Innuendo, body language, jokes, and even something as simple as laughter just escapes us! Sometimes people seem to laugh at what you're saying, even though you weren't trying to make them laugh. You weren't saying something funny in your head. And you'll say to them, 'That wasn't a joke, I'm being serious.'

You are participating in a genuine conversation, and you're giving your thoughts, opinions, or remarks and you didn't mean to make them laugh. This leads to uncomfortable feelings on both sides. Embarrassment and insecurity are feelings that follow.

Do you have dry humor? Wry humor? Dark humor? No humor? It seems to run together and look a lot like everything else, and it gets too complicated.

HER: Ben has frequently asked me, "Mom, why are you laughing? Was that funny? Can you explain that to me?" My poor, dear Ben. It's hit and miss. He doesn't know what is and isn't funny.

HIM: People tell me I can be naturally funny; I can make people laugh. But even within my family I am questioned, 'Was that a joke?' Our family had a dear friend, Paula, and when I was being irreverent, sarcastic, or flippant, she would laugh. Most of the time I didn't realize that what I said would be perceived that way. I was just 'shooting from the cuff' and couldn't have done that on purpose if I had tried. More often than not, it usually goes the opposite way and I end up offending someone or embarrassing myself.

This is exactly why I prefer to observe and not get involved because the last thing I want to do is bring negative attention to myself. That's the absolute worst.

I frequently find if I'm trying to be funny, it doesn't work. Sometimes when I make a comment, I'm unintentionally clever and I make people laugh. And then I'm confused because I simply cannot recreate it deliberately, and I didn't do it on purpose.

HER: While at a training meeting today, a woman was sharing a good story. She stopped momentarily and mentioned that she had wanted to use our names, from our nametags, as part of the story, but because she was mostly blind she couldn't see the writing. It just looked like a bunch of squiggles and lines to her.

Ben pipes up, "But…isn't that what writing…is?"

Everyone in the room laughed, and she moved on with her story. Afterwards Ben came to me. "I don't understand, why did everyone laugh?"

And so, I explained. Ben still doesn't really get it, but I thought it was hilarious.

INSIGHT: It would seem that what works is accidental, and what's intentional falls flat. This creates a frustrating, paralyzing paradox. The inability to replicate these moments of unintentional wit underscores a deeper challenge — a disconnect between internal intention and external reception. For many neurodivergent individuals, this showcases the broader struggle found while navigating social dynamics. Humor is unpredictable and inconsistent and is just one more thing that cannot be trusted.

17 Eye Contact is Uncomfortable

CHALLENGE: In many cultures, eye contact is seen as a sign of attention, interest, and trust. So, for some people, it helps form connections. But for others — especially autistic folks or those with social anxiety — eye contact can feel intense, uncomfortable, and overwhelming.

You can't blame the autistic person. If you want to connect with someone whose brain works differently, you'll need to change your approach – the usual way of greeting people might not work the same.

HIM: Looking you in the eye is uncomfortable for me—it's too intense. This is seen as a failure to connect with people, but more specifically, others seem to struggle to connect with me. Before I met Diana, my daughters had a dear friend. She got to know my girls through the local church program. At one point she told me, 'If it hadn't been for your girls, I would never have gotten to know you. Your face, your body language just felt so unapproachable.' Because of my autism I came across to others as too distant or detached. I don't really understand what that means. I don't wear an aloof face on purpose. But apparently, there it is.

My son, Ben, seems to have the same issue. However, it is multiplied. His 'resting face' is quite intimidating and he even looks angry, glaring at the world without knowing that's how it looks.

INSIGHT: If you see us as quirky, weird, strange, or odd, it may be that we are. Be patient enough to give us a chance. Be adventurous enough to say hello, inquisitive enough to ask a couple of questions, and brave enough to see if we've got enough in common to strike up a friendship. Friendship isn't built on one behavior alone. It's built on mutual respect, shared interests, consistency, and kindness. If eye contact doesn't come naturally, that's okay—there are plenty of other ways to connect.

You may have just made the most wonderful discovery!

18 | Viewing the World From Afar

CHALLENGE: Some people enjoy people-watching — sitting quietly in a café or shop, just observing the world like it's a live TV show. For some autistic individuals, this can be a comfortable way to connect with the world: by watching from a distance, without needing to interact. It's a form of connection that feels safe, controlled, and on their own terms. And for some, that works best.

HIM: My professor gave me an assignment to just observe people for several days. I tried, I really did, but I just sort of felt 'creepy,' sitting there watching people.

HER: For the longest time I kept taking Ben (and James) to events in town ranging from the water park to the Christmas performance of The Nutcracker. Sometimes an event would land James in bed with a migraine for days. Ben would become even more protective of his time, in his space, with his computer. I couldn't understand until very recently that attending these events wasn't fun for them. I thought I was providing the very best enriching experiences, yet in truth only exposed them to experiences that taught them what they didn't like instead. That's not necessarily bad information, but definitely not what I had in mind. I wanted shared, happy memories. Nope, wasn't happening.

James' needs are much more simply met and sound like the perfect ad from a dating app. 'Love quiet evenings, simple food, and going on walks.' Then the small print would read, "...on my own timeline and terms."

When dating a man with autism, make sure to discover the addendums to the relationship, realizing they might not know what those are at the beginning either.

When you're like James, you prefer to observe rather than interact. He says if he opens his mouth he generally ends up embarrassing himself. If you're like me, this is where I need to learn to let go. I still struggle with this. I tend to want to take my spouse and children to events, concerts, museums, plays, etc., to 'expand their horizons' like my mom did for me. However, Ben has informed me that he doesn't like to go to any of these places because there are crowds, too many flashing lights, way too much noise, and people everywhere. It is physically painful for Ben and James to attend certain events. I didn't realize I was adding to overstimulated sensory issues, creating heightened feelings of anxiety and stress which led to sleep disturbances, mood swings, and decreased mental well-being. *Wow.* Give them the benefit of the doubt; believe.

JEN: I remember my brother, Ben, desperately needing smaller spaces ever since he was little. The world was all around him, enormous, as he walked to and from school. To combat this feeling of overwhelm even as a teen, he would deliberately wear a hoodie, pulled up tight and scrunched close so that his view was restricted to tunnel vision. This made the trek more bearable. At this time, he was still terrified someone would shoot him. Oddly, wearing a hoodie helped him feel safer.

INSIGHT: Neurotypical expectations for what a well-rounded life looks like and the reality of what an autistic person can endure are two entirely different things. Let go and trust that what they tell you they need is, in fact, accurate.

19 Authority issues

CHALLENGE: It's common for some children and adults on the autism spectrum to respond to authority in ways that might seem challenging. This can include things like not following instructions, appearing to ignore requests, or showing signs of frustration through aggressive behavior. Often, these reactions aren't about defiance, but about difficulty coping with stress, sensory overload, or communication barriers. In some cases, that stress may lead to behaviors that seem socially inappropriate, but they're usually signals of deeper discomfort or unmet needs.

HER: One of the most endearing memories I have is when Ben was recovering from a dentist's anesthesia. The dental intern and I helped him into a recovery room and made sure he was comfortable with a blanket. He was still 'out.' As he began to stir, he started to mumble, "I don't like this." Then he tried to sit up, nearly falling on the floor. The intern made sure Ben was safe as he tried to regain control of his extremities. Ben would throw his arm in the air to help turn himself over. "Children should be in charge!" he shouted into the room. "We know what we need, not parents. I know what I want to eat…hot dogs." He would rest for a while, then sit up with a start proclaiming, "I think kids should be in charge. Why is it always her?!" and he pointed at me. "We should make the rules, they would make more sense!" This lasted for the forty-five minutes or so it took for the drugs to wear off. I must admit, they really loosened up his tongue.

There are a few common reasons why this reaction to authority might show up.

- **Transitions**: Shifting from one activity to another can be tough. Sometimes, it's simply that they don't want to stop doing what they're currently focused on.

- **Sensory overstimulation**: The environment might be too much — too bright, too loud, too chaotic. For example, Ben gets really irritated when the mirror lights are on while brushing his teeth. He's tall, so the lights hit him right at eye level, and I get it — that would be uncomfortable for anyone.

- **Perceived unfairness**: Sometimes, it's just the sense that something feels unjust or arbitrary, and that frustration comes out in their behavior.

HER: When Ben was in middle school, there was a lot going on at home. James had recently been temporarily paralyzed by some depression medication, and after the initial months of his care, I needed to go to work to support the family. One day I got a call and was asked to get up to the middle school as quickly as I could. I was told Ben had a difference of opinion with the principal and had locked him out of the school. Yes, he actually did that!

Apparently as the principal was making his rounds behind the school, he saw several boys playing with some large sticks. He told the boys they needed to put them down for safety's sake. Most obeyed, but Ben was annoyed. He was enjoying the game. He kind of growled at the principal. Now, everyone in the school knew Ben. They liked him and generally understood his different approach to things. He eventually put the stick down and followed the principal around for a moment or two and then went on his way. Ben had gone inside the school, and locked the doors so the principal couldn't get back in.

I arrived quickly and found my son in one of the counseling rooms pacing back and forth and as agitated as could be. At this time, there was always an essential oil roller bottle of Wild Orange and Douglas Fir in either his backpack or my purse. I sat him down in an office chair, knee to knee, pulled out my essential oils and began to give him an Aromatouch hand massage. I was able to calm him down very quickly, and then we were able to talk. Sometimes a good aroma, some gentle hand massaging, and a calm voice can work miracles. Ben really, really doesn't care for those who have more authority than he does. We were lucky to work it all out amicably.

INSIGHTS: It is best to carry a few items on your person to help diffuse intense situations. Figuring out what works for your loved one is paramount since we all respond so differently to distress.

20 Mental FOG

CHALLENGE: Brain fog is a collection of symptoms that can affect those on the spectrum. In children it might look like 'zoning out,' while in adults it can make it difficult to learn or remember. It reduces the mental process or cognition needed to acquire knowledge and understanding through thought, experience, and one's senses.

So, what is an example of cognition? It would include *paying attention to something in the environment*, learning something new, making decisions, processing language, solving problems, using memory, and *being aware of things in the spaces around you*, e.g. environmental stimuli.

HER: I call it walking in a fog which may sound a little vague. However, James says this, "When we decide to walk from where we are to say the bathroom on the other side of the house, we picture it in our mind, and we go there. We don't notice stuff in between."

HER: I should have keyed on his words ...picture it in our mind. "How can you *not* notice that pile of towels? You *know* they belong in the bathroom and you could have taken them with you on the way."

HIM: "Well, it's irrelevant to our plan. Basically, it's a peripheral, it doesn't exist. Now, movement might catch our attention, but something just sitting there—nope, not happening."

HER: This last weekend we were with the family for a 'cousin's camp.' After the festivities and cooking were done for the day, I asked Ben to please use a few rags and clean up the kitchen floor. He looked at me perplexed and confused.

BEN: "Why?"

HER: "Ben, it is covered in dirt, juices and other things that have turned to muddy splotches all over. It needs to be put to rights. It needs to shine. It will help create joy in your mother and your sisters." He clomped away to get the cleaning rags.

BEN: As he returned he began, "Mom, I just don't get it. I walk around with my eyes straight forward. I get where I want to go, and everything looks fine to me. I never even notice stuff like this! What do you do, walk around with your eyes always on the floor and on the walls? How is it you don't fall down all the time? How is it you always see the spiders in the corner, or the stray earwig, or notice trash needs to be removed? I just don't get it. I *never* see this stuff."

HER: Ben is not usually this articulate. I had really struck a nerve today. I simply replied, "Ben, there are germs all around on things I'm responsible to keep clean so that my family doesn't die. We're on a cattle farm. People play with the cats, dogs, and calves and ride the four-wheelers goodness knows where. Some of those outside germs are on the floor with the spilled food. Ben, please trust me on this, and mop the floor." He just stared at me, and then mumbled, "Sure thing." He laid into it with great energy and had that floor shining in no time, but wow, I will not soon forget his tirade.

From my point of view, learning to deal with their brain fog was hard. Jen has suffered even within the family because of our steep learning curve over time which ranged from not understanding how very real this mental space is, to accepting her as well as embracing, loving and including her in spite of it. The only one at the beginning who really dug in (because she loved the way Jen thought) was her sister, Em. God bless Em for being there for Jen. I never stopped trying, but *oh* those 'gaining grey hair moments' kept coming. At last, I began to see the light. It made life *so* much better for us both.

I remember being at my mother-in-law's funeral and trying to explain to Jen's older sisters why she wasn't responding immediately to questions they asked her at breakfast. I told them she needed a little more time to process information than we did and she would answer them when she was ready. The oldest sister got angry and said that I might have time to sit around waiting but she didn't have the time or desire to learn a new skill and how ridiculous it was. This situation escalated later in the day when the same sister came storming into our hotel room. I looked up and saw the sparks flying everywhere. As an NT, I could 'read the room' and it was a doozy! Jen looked up and happily said, "Oh, hi!" She did not see or recognize the emotion pouring off her sister.

I cannot print most of this story. Suffice it to say: in relationships, sensitivity is critical, while rigid non-acceptance and violence are the death blow. So much was lost because of misunderstanding, lack of acceptance, and lack of love and compassion. This precious daughter was on the edge. The situation became out of control over a disagreement that could have been resolved so very differently.

If Jen had been allowed time to think she might have worded things differently. Had 'sister' been less irritable and not so easily offended, she would have seen the longing in Jen's eyes and understood she meant no offense.

Jen bore bruises for days following this incident. Their relationship has never been the same. James and Jen were vibrating on a frequency that was both horrifying and sad at the same time. I'm sure 'sister' was too. This is where James says I 'peeled them off the ceiling.' I often bring out my essential oils when emotions run amok. I'm grateful we had them with us that day.

If you'd like further information about essential oils and how they can support emotional and mental health, please feel free to contact me.

HER: Within the realm of our Yours, Mine and Ours family of eleven, it is amazing to see the varying degrees of flexibility and rigidity that exist. Those who have learned to bend, accept and adapt have a much more relaxed relationship with each other.

Ben spoke with me today and mentioned that sometimes he

thinks the family would operate more easily without him in the mix. I looked at him for a moment. "Ben. Think about those you know in our family with autism, or some type of disability. Dad, you, Rowan, Jen, Em, Ace, Mara, Mel, Iris, Nat, Owen, Tiffa, Zac (this includes three generations). How interesting would our lives be if these people weren't in our family?" He thought for a moment and said, "I guess it would be kind of bland, not very interesting. Not spicy enough, huh?"

HIM: Brain Fog: It feels like I'm lost in a mist, or a heavy, blinding tule fog all the time. Was I cursed at birth? Why can't I think clearly like others I know? (I must admit I'm so envious.) I spend so much time working over problems to find solutions and end up in a dead end in life's figurative maze. I see others making 3D art projects and STL files. I bought a 3D printer but could never figure out how to tweak it correctly, it just fried my brain. Is this just more of my mathematics problem? I'm not sure. I have no idea how to explain it. The hierarchy of a computer just confuses me. I lose track of all that. When I have it written down, I seem to stumble through it, but remembering it easily is as difficult as trying to remember those plays when I was on the high school football team.

HER: I remember one night in particular after James spent several days working with DAZ studio, trying to get the lighting right. He came to me and lamented, "I can't seem to think my way out of a paper bag!" He had called the company and been told there were no tutorials or in-class teaching opportunities for this. They don't support it that way. The tutorials seem to be geared for people who know a certain level of operation already. James would need a beginner's level training video he could play repetitively, with no assumption of previous knowledge, until it stuck. James has figured out basic autoCAD, and would love to learn 3DStudio Max. However, his learning style would require something he simply hasn't discovered yet. He has no idea how to explain why he can understand certain things, and others escape him entirely.

HIM: Healthy comfort food makes a lot of things better. It's interesting what constitutes healthy comfort food. Make sure you have prepared some to have on hand for the times you're out or feeling the need to snack at home. I love a good handful of pecans, for one.

HER: One day, when James was on the road driving a truck, I received a phone call. He didn't say hello, or how are you, or how's your day been. He blurted out, "You have Ruined. My. Life!" I responded, "What? What have I done?"

HIM: "Remember how you asked me to have a salad every day? You said I could eat all my same foods, but to please add just one salad every day."

HER: "Yes, I remember that. I was also giving you a cup of fresh carrot/apple/celery juice when you were home, but that's all."

HIM: "Well, I'm here at this truck stop surrounded by food I used to eat. I don't want *any* of it, and there is not a salad to be seen. You've ruined my life!"

HER: "I don't know what to say…"

HIM: And then he started laughing. "I'm messing with you, but there isn't any green food to be had. I'm really missing it."

INSIGHT: Don't give up! Our suggestions in this subject matter involve deliberate, intentional self-care. These points of care support better brain function.

- **Sleep makes a person feel more mentally clear.** This is hard to get when you have a sleep disorder, but the message is the same. Get as much regular sleep as you can.

- **Get some exercise every day.** Moving the body to get some blood flowing is essential to heart health. Try something new, perhaps flexibility stretches, yoga, walking or swimming. One of *her* favorite ways to get the blood pumping is simple belly-dancing.

- **Remain hydrated.** A dehydrated body leads to constipation and illness. Proper water intake keeps the pipes running smoothly.

- **Eat a healthy diet with balanced amounts of colorful veggies.** If you can't stand the "chewing," please consider smoothies in an array of different colors. They nourish various body systems and help with health and vitality.

DEEPER INSIGHT: Don't give up! Continue to seek the things you need. If the above habits are in place for optimal health and well-being on a physical level, there is a pro-active step that needs to be taken next. It's time to look for the accommodations that are needed to facilitate success. This may help you have the support you need as you move forward. To illustrate, we're going to focus on what you might need to learn a specific computer program.

- **Know Your Needs:**
    - What is it I wish to learn? (autoCAD, DAZ3d, etc.)
    - What are my end goals?

- What specific challenges are you facing with the program. Is it the layout, the hierarchy, the instructions, or perhaps the pace of learning? Identifying these will help you request targeted support

- **Identify the Right Person:** Contact the relevant department—this might be Disability Services (in a school) or HR/IT support (at work or the business you're looking into) If you're uncertain, ask who handles accommodation requests.

- **Prepare Your Request:** Be clear and constructive. You don't need to disclose everything about your autism/disability. Mention that you have a learning difference and require accommodations. This will help you frame the conversation.

- **Questions to Ask:**

  - Are there accommodations available for neurodivergent individuals?

  - Can I get step-by-step written instructions for this program?

  - Is there a way to adjust the interface for better accessibility (e.g., changing colors, fonts, or contrast)?

  - Could I have extra time to complete tasks while learning the program?

  - Is it possible to have a point of contact or mentor to assist when I get stuck?

  - Are there video tutorials or alternate formats for the training materials?

  - Can I get creative in a 'sandbox' environment to learn without consequences for mistakes?

- Follow Up: If you haven't heard back, follow up. Once accommodations are set, check in as you work through it. Communication both ways is key.

- Evaluate: Were you able to attain your goal?
    - What further questions could be asked if you seek better results?
    - What steps are needed to achieve this goal?
    - Has my learning style affected the outcome?

        One grandchild has discovered the delights of speech-to-text software. What a gift! It helped her organize her thoughts, keep lists, and write her very first cohesive story.

- Celebrate your new skill set!

21 Caregiver Burnout

CHALLENGE: Caregiver burnout is a state of mental, physical, and emotional exhaustion that can happen when you dedicate your life (time and energy) to managing someone else's health and safety and frequently ignoring your own. Stressed-out caregivers may experience anxiety, fatigue, and depression. This category includes so much more than the ND-NT relationship we have been exploring up until now. We include new mothers, new fathers, those who care for their aging parents, and those that care for property management businesses. If your business is helping people, you are at risk for overload, overwhelm, overdone, then overcome.

HER: What about my own needs? Not just dreams, desires and hopes, but true needs. I've become really good at measuring and meeting the needs of others, spouse and children. But what about mine? There must be a balance here that won't leave me feeling unfulfilled, empty, lonely, lost, desperate, and yet not cross into the realm of guilt when I take care of myself. I'm a caregiver in this situation, but I'm also a wife, or supposed to be. There is such a disparity…

The signs and symptoms of caregiver burnout are similar to those of stress and depression.

- Emotional, mental, and physical exhaustion
- Feeling hopeless and helpless
- Changes in sleep patterns
- Inability to concentrate
- Getting sick more often
- Irritability, frustration or anger toward others

You can reduce your risk of burnout by participating in respite care.

HER: The solutions for appropriate personal care when dealing with caretaker burnout are as varied as our caretakers. Sometimes all we need is a few hours in a pool, by ourselves. Sometimes all we need is a mini-vacation, or a slightly longer one. Sometimes, we have to carefully evaluate and judge the distress and let the job go.

You are the one that knows you best. You are the best judge for what you need, and what you can continue to manage in your life. Carefully, prayerfully consider your needs, and move ahead accordingly, without guilt.

Golden Nuggets to ensure you, too, have a healthy well-being.

1. Make time for self-care, such as taking a rest day, going for a walk and doing things that make you feel relaxed and happy.

2. Avoid feeling low-spirited. Go out and meet other people to help relieve stress and loneliness. Know yourself.

3. When it gets hard, learn to lean into or ask others for support. Another family member, a friend, or an organization can often help you 'expand your horizons' with ideas you hadn't thought about on your own.

Thinking about being healthy doesn't do a thing for you until you take that first step, followed by another, and then practicing consistency. You may consider talking with a mental health professional as well.

Create a personal accountability chart—there are many online to choose from.

Choose an accountability partner, and a system that works for you.

I have brothers who had a goal. They would report in every night, being accountable for doing the self-care things they said they would do. If they had not drunk the required water, and not completed the required exercise, and not eaten the healthy food, then they would owe $100 to the other brother for that day, payable at the end of the week. Then, they ended every week with a phone call.

INSIGHT: Being a caregiver can lead to self-neglect. You can reduce your risk of burnout by knowing more about respite care, finding a support group, and actually doing self-care instead of just thinking about it. Wait, is that really a thing? Am I allowed to do that? *whispers* Am I important enough to take the time, for myself?!

Speaking from experience: yes it is, and yes you are!

22 | Reciprocity

HER: We've begun every section with a stated challenge, but here we wish to reiterate that the following opinions and stories are directly from our lives together and are in no way inferring that all NT-ND relationships will be filled with this specific level of inequity and misunderstanding, and yet still try to function. Your experiences will depend on the depth of your diagnosis, and level of cognitive function involved for both partners, your commitment, and your personalities.

THE DREAM: When two people have equal exchange of goods or services, they are enjoying reciprocity, a situation where each enjoys an equal benefit from the relationship.

CHALLENGE: The 'Dream' is also the challenge.

This is truly a profound statement. In a ND-NT marriage, achieving reciprocity will be complex because each partner will experience and express needs, emotions (or lack of emotion) and support in very different ways. The 'dream' is a relationship where both partners feel understood, valued, and supported—a true partnership of equals. The 'challenge' lies in bridging the gap between different communication styles, expectations, and way of processing the world.

Marriage/Partnerships takes patience, intentional communication and a willingness to learn each other's perspectives. When done right with true awareness from both parties, our differences can actually enrich the relationship, fostering deeper empathy and unique problem-solving approaches. We've discussed how much an NT needs to adapt and adjust to make things work. In this section, it should be obvious that ND persons *also* need to be open to being corrected, re-directed, and counseled. If these traits are not evident, the relationship *will* suffer.

HER: The trouble is, just reading the above paragraph creates complex issues when paired with the memories of the last twenty-five years. I've struggled through perplexing, puzzling, tangled, tortuous, baffling, elaborate conversations that ended up with him not having said much of anything at all that I could get my hooks into. It's like trying to eat steak with a straw.

I've had thirty-minute conversations that when referenced later in the month, are not even remembered except for a vague half-sentence. One specifically had been a really, really important conversation involving marriage, housing, my breaking heart, etc. This was complicated at the time by his seven-month recovery from COVID, the doctor's recommendation that he walk in sunshine every day, laugh and interact with the grandchildren, and have no stress in his life other than getting well, and the need for me to create excellent nutrition in the foods he could eat. Ben was also recovering from a longer illness at the time.

Technically, I'm married — but the loneliness has grown over time, especially as our conversations have dwindled in areas we used to share. In more than twenty-four years together, there's rarely been a sense of true reciprocity. And now, as he's embraced his autism and understanding of himself, his boundaries around conversation have only tightened. Topics we used to enjoy are now off-limits, and places we once went together are no longer part of our lives. The distance has deepened, not just physically, but emotionally.

This book needed to acknowledge his personal growth while still honoring my emotional truth — the loss of shared space and connection. My hope is that it conveys both the reality of my loneliness and the complexity of his journey, without diminishing either.

When he needs to talk about his art, his models, the humor

he finds in certain video feeds, music, or mold creation—I am there to listen. But his ability to listen to me is extremely limited.

My Aunt Barbara and my mother used to go traveling together for about two weeks every year. One year they went to Jamaica, and the next visited Banff, Canada. Then they spent time in England learning to make ceramic dishes, you know the ones from Staffordshire that specialize in blue dishes. These sisters have fabulous memories together. Why? Because they planned together-time, which also gave their husbands down time, too. (Not to mention the downtime *from* their husbands and kids) They thoroughly enjoyed their separate vacations, exploring both new and old hobbies.

INSIGHT: Find the solution that works for you, for your partnership. I'm still trying to figure out a good solution for this dilemma.

23 Gullibility and Innocence

CHALLENGE: It is a sad, sad place we live when those who are most vulnerable are taken advantage of, stolen from, deceived and then end up feeling it is *their* error for being the butt of the thief's deceit. Addressing the challenge of gullibility and risk of being scammed in autism requires a multifaceted approach, with a focus on support, education, and empowerment.

For our purposes, innocence means the state of being inexperienced, lacking sophistication, or simply naive. Gullible means being easily deceived or tricked into trusting someone.

James nearly lost his life during the COVID pandemic. He was one of those with lung issues, ended up hospitalized and endured a long recovery at home afterwards, twice. As he slowly regained his health he wanted to contribute to supporting the family again, so he became an Uber driver. He'd worked for about a week and had nearly $500 in his account. He was excited for payday. Then, he got a call. He thought it was from corporate. Long story short, by the end of the call they wiped out his account. When he figured it out, there was nothing anyone could do. He had been scammed—and lost. All the wind was sucked from his sails. He couldn't understand why someone would do that.

In various arenas, this has happened multiple times. He believes people. He gets scammed every few years. It is frustrating for him and ultimately disheartening and discouraging. It contributes to his 'burnout' events, when he won't leave the shop in the basement—his creative 'safe' space.

INSIGHT: We can talk about how scams work and teach about the tactics scammers use with structured lessons, role-playing or examples. Awareness about these red flags may help develop a sense of caution. However, when you know that trust is ever present, and there is no natural 'stranger danger,' this approach is not the most effective, even though it's usually the first mentioned.

We can make sure there is a structured support system in place where someone else may need to be contacted prior to making purchases or moving money around. A list of reliable contacts in that moment of stress may help in making wiser decisions.

Digging deeper may require not just a suggested support system but clear boundaries with limits on how much money can be spent without consulting someone or knowing that certain financial decisions require a second opinion from someone he trusts before committing.

A lot of autistic individuals thrive on predictability and routine. If you get scammed and feel disheartened by it, it may be helpful to create positive routines that include regular check-ins or a system where they're encouraged to reflect on their decisions or actions.

Remember to address the emotional impact of being scammed. Scams feel like betrayal, leading to feelings of shame, discouragement, and worthlessness. Knowledge of coping mechanisms, such as stress management or self-compassion techniques to help deal with feelings of frustration when something goes wrong, may be helpful.

After one of these incidents, finding ways to channel creativity and self-expression may reduce burnout and give more control over personal emotional responses. Hopefully, these strategies would help protect against future scams while also supporting emotional well-being.

24 Privileges are NOT rights

CHALLENGE: Driving requires a blend of several important skills not limited to vehicle control, traffic awareness, defensive driving and navigation. All of this must happen while adhering to traffic laws and regulations.

HER: When children are about sixteen, society tries to give every one of them a driver's license. I have helped nine children obtain this privilege. The most frightening moment as I taught one daughter about the necessary skills was when I said, "Now, sweetheart, it is important that when you pass a road you look right and left to make sure you are safe." I was saying this on a country road, far from the busy streets in town. She responded by saying, "What street?"

Ah, I see. At this point, I told her she wasn't ready to receive a license because she wasn't aware enough of her environment and surroundings. I refused to teach her further until she 'grew into adulthood' just a bit more. About a year later, her stepdad tried to teach her. It didn't go well as she ended up going the wrong way into a busy freeway exit near San Diego. He, too, refused to teach her further. She travelled the world, went to Japan, had a few life's experiences, and learned about many public transportation options.

A few years later, I received a phone call. She wanted to come home. We worked out the details. There were some strict boundaries put in place. After a time, she decided to try to get her license again. She needed thirty hours of daytime practice. She asked me to help her accomplish this goal. The best part of this story, from her perspective, is my request that if I was going to spend my time helping her reach this goal, that she would drive me to various graveyards in the valley so I could help take photos and document them. She agreed! And so, we achieved two goals, together. How old was she then? About twenty-four. It took nine additional years for her to obtain this coveted I.D. And she was finally ready, more aware, and far more cognizant of the responsibility.

Ben had no desire to drive. At all. Nada. We did some basic training and he managed to take out a mail box. He wasn't ready. He was so relieved. Sixteen came and went, then seventeen and eighteen. I'm grateful there is no mandatory time for this privilege to be acquired.

"Ben, why don't you want to drive?"

"Mom, it's not like a video game. It's dangerous, people could really get hurt, and there is *no* reset button so I can start over without damages." Nineteen, then twenty, and twenty-one.

"Ben, I think it might be a good idea to try again. The

cannery where you volunteer could use some fork-lift drivers, and you can't do that training unless you have your license. What do you think?"

It took us over a year to accomplish this goal. He has his license and knows this is a skill set he can use for various purposes, but he still prefers not to drive on city streets.

INSIGHT: We have established that those with autism are often several years behind their peers in social and cognitive development. If one does not have the ability to judge distances and identify potential road hazards and conditions, then one shouldn't be behind the wheel of a vehicle.

25 Another 'Lack of Connection'

CHALLENGE 1: In addition to a lack of connection to the people surrounding them, there is the same lack of connection to their roots, their family history. My autistic spouse can't understand what he *can* see, let alone how to connect to what he can't see.

So, how did he gain a genuine bond with his family tree? He has a love for history. We were able to obtain much of his dad's military records and discovered his heroism in battle. We continued researching his Catlin line. We found men in every action all the way back to the Revolutionary War. His favorite story is how his 2x great-grandfather served the Union forces and ended up a prisoner of war in Salisbury, North Carolina. Just a few months prior to the end of the war, he died in that camp. His great-grandfather was not quite three years old at the time.

The interesting part of this story is obtained from the military records on his mother's side of the family. There was a camp commander with the last name of Gee who was given the thankless task of running this camp in Salisbury near the end of the war. He was tried for war crimes and acquitted. His camp swelled to unmanageable numbers and prisoners died in the cold, impossible conditions. It's a truly tragic story.

Now, James doesn't do paperwork, no, not ever. He won't be found thumbing through the virtual paper piles seeking his family roots and their stories. But when a story is brought to his attention and he can put the story into an historical construct, lights go on. His response to the above story, "Wow. They say this is the war that brother fought brother, the tragic reality of the American Civil War. And there they are! My ancestors, a cousin on my mom's side and my 2nd great-grandfather on dad's side, killing each other."

For him, the blending of a 'family name' which meant nothing at the start, was brought to life when paired with real historical events. This is one avenue which may help your autistic person forge a bridge between themselves and their past.

CHALLENGE 2: Feeling 'less than,' because as an ND you recognize that your wiring is not as well-organized or as effective as someone else.

Ben came to me today. "Mom, I feel so inferior. How can I ever measure up? I know people who can knock a conversation out of the park, landing several 'home runs' before I can figure out where the topic is going, and then just when I figure out how to contribute, everything switches tracks and I'm left in the dust again, trying to add something of value to the conversation.

"I feel my 'difference,' but have no idea how to adjust the dials on my out-of-date, old-style radio. Everyone else seems to have the latest, greatest mental apps for streaming multiple programs, and I struggle to get my wiring to recognize the 'on' switch."

HER: At this point, my hearing became laser focused. My son, who rarely talks about anything except computer games, and *that* with incomplete sentences, reached out with a deeply tender broken heart. He struggles with self-esteem, and today he decided to talk about it. He opened up. This showed remarkable trust and emotional intelligence.

I could have given him a platitude: "Don't worry, everything will be fine." or "You can do it, I believe in you." This would not be what he needed right now. The underlying message was, "I'm afraid. I don't feel equal to the task. What could my voice add that someone else hasn't already said, and said it better? How do I know when to talk?"

All of those feelings and questions came through as his tears ran down his face. As he embraces his chosen volunteer work, he's coming face-to-face with what life will require of him. There are new skills he needs to learn. This is good. It is also good that he can ask questions when he figures out what he wants to say. I didn't want to offer simple, easy reassurance. At this moment, when he reached out for help, this was the time to offer the skill set (sometimes called an accommodation) I knew would help him. Information he wasn't ready for, until now. He then went to his room for a while, to pace, to think, play video games and process.

One of the benefits of working with my autistic children is the time they need to 'process.' It lets me work fast and furiously to create my own brand of magic. Of course, as any self-respecting mom nowadays, I turned to Google for help. I wanted to reframe his narrative to help boost his self-esteem but do it with a little humor and maybe some class. These topics for conversation were discussed when he was ready.

Ben mentioned how he felt like a malfunctioning radio. We considered the following possibilities:

- **Embrace Your Vintage Vibes**
  - Who needs the latest apps when you've got a classic? Your mind isn't outdated—it's retro! Vintage radios may take a little extra tuning, but when they pick up a signal, the sound is rich, warm and unforgettable.

- **Reframe the 'On' Switch Struggle**
  - Sometimes the 'on' switch isn't faulty, it's just in an unexpected place. Maybe your brain works more like an escape room. You've got to pull the right levers, decode a few clues, and occasionally flip a metaphorical table before the lightbulb flickers on. When it does? Magic.

- **Secret Superpower**
  - Remember, new apps are often buggy. Your mind's unique wiring gives you perspectives others can't even download. Sure, it takes longer to load sometimes, but when it does, you're running a custom

OS built for creativity, resilience, and unexpected brilliance.

We had some good laughs and were able to move on to some practical strategies. Next, it was wonderful to share some of the things I had learned long ago in Toastmaster classes.

- **The Power of Pause**
  - Not everyone needs to be a fast talker to be a great conversationalist. Thoughtful contributions are often the most impactful. You're not 'left in the dust.' You're the one carefully observing and choosing your words with intention.

- **Conversation is a Team Sport**
  - Home runs are flashy, but every great team needs players who keep the game steady and bring new perspectives. You might not be swinging for the fences every second, but when you step up to the plate, your insight could be what changes the whole game.

- **Silent Superpower**
  - Being a good listener is rare. Your ability to notice when the conversation shifts and think before speaking means you're probably picking up details others miss. That's a strength, not a weakness.

In a conversation, when you want a little more time to gather your thoughts, you may want to use the following conversation anchors. Things like, "That's really interesting. Can you tell me more about that?" or "I never thought of it that way. What made you see it like that?" In this way you have participated, shown genuine interest, and yet you don't have to do the talking.

Sometimes, communication isn't about words. It's about body language (and yes, we've had this discussion in a previous chapter. Even though it is not a natural, inherent skill set, if he wants to learn, it is possible to pick up a few things). Nodding, smiling, or giving a thoughtful 'hmm' shows engagement and participation. Sometimes, presence speaks louder than anything else.

Sometimes it is okay to circle back to a previous part of the discussion. If you think of something you could add later, you might say, "I've been thinking about what you said earlier, and…" This simple sentence helps you segue to a previous item and shows you were paying attention, which may add depth to the discussion.

As our conversation wandered through laughter, hugs, and contemplative moments. I told him how proud of him I was. He told me he didn't want to be a failure and again stated how he feels stuck on a narrow band and keeps trying to find the frequency other people are using, and that most of the time, he fails. But then he also said he had learned that 'comparison was the father of defeat,' of course restating Theodore Roosevelt's statement 'Comparison is the thief of joy.' "I want to learn. I want to grow, it's just so hard to figure it out." Ben's young niece heard some of this conversation and stated, "But I think Uncle is perfect!"

BEN: "Mom! I've always hated the way the school tried to teach me about learning and growing and used the 'flexible' and 'inflexible' brain analogy. I much prefer how Dehaka from the Star Craft II game talks about it. 'We need to be an entity that adapts, changes, and moves. You can't be a rock, you can't be a stone, a tree or a hill. You can't be any of these things. You will be knocked down. You need to be capable of ebbing and flowing.' That's what I think about when I need to learn something new."

HER: What an interesting evening this evolved into! Have you ever tried to teach public speaking tips and self-confidence through the lens of a Star Craft Game? It was epic, educational, and delightful.

CHALLENGE 3: There is often a disconnect and mental conflict between the needs of the family, of the bigger picture, being a team player, and the autistic one's own need for stability and perceived safety.

This 'shared space dilemma' highlights the emotional and physical tug-of-war between personal comfort zones and the shared demands of family life. It could also be called 'mutual needs negotiation;' a neutral, respectful term that captures the idea of both sides having valid needs that must be balanced thoughtfully. I prefer 'compassionate compromise' in which we see the importance of empathy from all sides, not just practical solutions.

In 2015, we needed to move North for Ben to receive the education he needed. I also needed help, being at the end of my rope since James was disabled so badly in Jan 2013. My daughter also needed help in her home, and this would move us closer to the VA hospital where I could get James what he needed within an hour, instead of a five-hour drive.

Note from Journal 2015: You won't move North. The room will be too small and unless all your tools can come with us, you aren't coming—not until I have an apartment for us, or the house is built. You *must* have your tools, or no go.

Did it ever occur to you that your son has needs at this time that are larger than yours? Did it ever occur to you that your needs have to be put on the back burner for a time? Did it ever cross your mind that you need to reach out to him, on his level, for the next six years until he is grown, so that he will develop into a better-functioning adult than is currently possible in our situation as it is right now? No, it hasn't. You're too mired in what you need, what you want, and what you think you must have. It's all about you. You are so sensitive to how you are treated by others (perceived) yet don't give a fig about how you treat them. You are…[hey, it's my journal, I called him out on his stuff, and called him names. For mental health, it's where you can vent without getting in trouble, or having to apologize later.] You don't even comprehend when you've been rude and said painful things. You lack tact, and you don't care about phrasing things so that they can be heard by another, in a softer way, so they will still want to be around you.

CHALLENGE 4: (Journal Musing 2005) When Nat was fourteen, I couldn't get her to do anything well, complete a chore or wash a dish so that it was actually clean. It was horrible. I'd had her for five years now. So, after all the charts, all the incentives, all the possible reward systems that the school told me to use, there had been *no* progress or growth. I was at my wits' end. Thus, one day I told her there was nothing to eat, and would be nothing to eat, until she finished her chores. (We're talking about making her bed, folding her own laundry, throwing away her bedtime diaper, and doing a few dishes, people. Not rocket science or hours of expectations.) Talk about the horror. She looked at me and literally said, "I never once in five years actually thought you meant it!"

All my tears. All my grey hair. All the instruction. All the concern. She never heard me, until I finally figured out what her motivation was. It was *food*!

CHALLENGE 5: (Journal Musing 2006) Tonight is the stuff of which a mother's crown of sorrow for having thought she had what it takes to be a mother, ever, is made of, I suppose. (Long, long day serving the family and my requests for assistance being ignored.) I fell asleep watching a show with Ben. James woke me, I stumbled to our bedroom, and that's when I saw it, all the clean laundry had been dumped at the end of my bed, hip deep. Nobody had bothered to fold it or put it away, as requested, while I drove them all over to lessons, classes, and events. I woke Em, Nat and Na. They began folding. Ro had been protected from many things for eighteen months due to her need for rest and long-term mono recovery, but now? Tonight, everyone was going to fold that laundry so I had a place to sleep. Anyway, Ro begins to bad-mouth me to the point the others can't stand to be in the room with her. She went on and on saying that I was being nitpicky, just looking for any old thing to deliberately pick on them. That I had no real reason to be demanding anything like this from them. Na asked her to stop being so negative, and she replied, "Why, I'm just being like mother." That's when Nat, Em and Na ended up in the kitchen, with me. That statement rates right up there with the time when she was in the seventh grade and told me, I was the biggest mistake her father had ever made. *Ouch.*

I needed support from James, but he just tells me that all teens behave in this brain-dead, selfish way and to quit having any expectations. I wish he'd help me teach his children that what they are doing is not acceptable. Mostly, he doesn't say a word because all he wants is peace. I ran all over today and had hoped for a little assistance and respect. I asked, "What about <u>my</u> needs?" He told me I'd better get used to the fact that his girls aren't going to help me, ever, because that isn't the nature of a teen. I just looked at him. I never treated my parents like this, Em and Na don't normally ignore their home responsibilities. So, all around, I'm to be treated like I'm the wicked person who just finds something useless to pick on them for, just for the sake of being nitpicky?! It really hurts to be so undervalued and only 'seen' when I can provide them with more of what they want.

I hurt…

CHALLENGE 6: Had Flat Tire – Family outings are filled with gaiety, chaos, laughter, joy, and sometimes challenges. When it gets overwhelming, sometimes the neurodivergent one 'checks out.' I had not learned this yet. We decided to take our little family on a trip to the Red Canyon, part of the Dixie National Forest, known for its stunning red rock formations. We managed to fit eight children into our van and begin our adventure. I decided to create sufficient room in the interior of the car and chose to remove the spare tire.

We had such a good time. We climbed, had lunch, hiked, laughed and took amazing photos. It was a splendid day. We put gasoline in the car, got ready to go home, and James drove over a curb. The tire complained, and split open. We were 'grounded.'

I asked James what we should do, since I had left the spare at home. He said he didn't know, leaned the driver's car seat into the reclining position, covered his face with a hat, and zoned out. That was it.

It was late. Businesses were mostly closed. I went down the road knocking on doors to find someone with a phone. I managed to contact a neighbor who would go to my home, get the tire off the porch, and bring it to us, about forty miles away. I called my friend, Michelle Ennis, who lived in LaVerkin at the time. She was actually in the process of moving that day, yet she took the time to come pick up all eight kids, take them to her home, feed them, and wait for me to put the car back together. Luckily when the tire arrived, James and my neighbor put things to rights, and we were able to pick up the children and make our way back home. It was a very, very long, frustrating day. I knew I had been surrounded by angels.

I asked James about that day in the coming years. I asked him why he had just covered his face and disappeared. That wasn't going to fix the problem. We needed to figure it out, work it through, get our family home. He told me he didn't know what to do, so he leaned back, closed his eyes, and stayed out of the way because he had nothing to contribute. I told him how abandoned I had felt, how utterly alone with the eight children and all their needs. There was fear, hunger, weariness, anxiety, potty runs with Ben, and he wasn't 'there.' He just shrugged his shoulders.

When the neurodivergent feel overwhelmed by circumstances, they will often 'check-out' and be 'unavailable' until things come back in to focus. This always left me feeling abandoned, and after all these years there are some PTSD issues for me. It is very difficult to go from "I'm out with my family and having a good time, so happy to be with my partner and our children," to: "maybe not, I thought I had a spouse, but looks like I've only got nine kids instead…"

CHALLENGE 7: Excerpt from Christmas Letter to the Family – 2013

Ben played soccer in the Spring. He had good team-mates, and an incredible coach. They worked with his Autism and made him feel like a very valuable member of the team.

Jennifer moved home in late August. She is continuing to go to school and discovering exactly what she can do. The professors are pleased with her efforts. Good Job, Jen!

Long story short: James—the doctors don't know what's wrong. He has had EEG's, MRI's, CT scans, blood work, etc. They don't know. The naturopath doesn't know. So, we go at life one day at a time and do the best we can.

Just a note: It is very, very challenging to know I'm relying on Jen for a few things. I rely on one with Asperger's, to help me with the other two with Asperger's/disability, while I work. This is stressful, and this is dangerous; here's why:

- She started a fire. She left the axe with the rubber handle on the Ben Franklin stove top. If that had caught fire, the home would have burned down.

- The sink clogged. She used the bathroom plunger in the kitchen sink. She didn't tell me it wasn't fixed, and that she'd used the bathroom plunger to try and unclog it. I also tried to unclog the sink with my hand in the disposal. When I turned it on, it spat droplets of water all over the kitchen. At this point, Jen informs me about the plunger. Consequently, I tell her we have to wash all the dishes again. She began to complain, "But I washed them before I used the plunger, they are clean." She couldn't seem to understand that they had to be washed because the disposal had spat the filthy, bathroom contaminated water all over, and insisted they were fine because she had washed them prior to the plunger's use. Her Asperger focus on the fact that she had done the dishes prior to the plunger wouldn't let her see the bigger picture *sigh* *another sigh* I sanitized the kitchen, and re-washed dishes.

- I've asked Jen why the kitchen isn't clean from time-to-time. She says, "But it is! I've finished the job." So, I take her to the kitchen and show her the counter with the dirty dishes still there. "Do you see this?" "Oh," she says. "I didn't see that before...." (This is nearly a daily occurrence...)

That's Jen, and these three incidents happened in a forty-five-minute time span, on one day. I never know, on a daily basis, what accident/disaster/problem I will have to deal with when I get home. Sometimes it's really hard to keep my temper, but I've learned to assess the situation, take a deep breath, take a deep breath again and speak calmly to address whatever it is I have to handle.

There are times that my head *is* wrapped appropriately around the idea that they just don't notice things and so don't function properly. These are actually the best of times, because you can sit back and just enjoy the time you have together, laughing with them and silently enjoying the things that just don't make sense.

I thank Heavenly Father for our home, our health, and our safety—daily. I'm glad to be alive, and glad to have the strength I have to care for others. God has richly blessed me.

So that's just a 'tip-of-the-iceberg' update for you.

Love,
Diana, Mother, Aunt Diana, Sister, Friend, etc.

CONCLUSION:

HIM/HER: In conclusion, *Autism and the Quest for Friendship: Echoes of Isolation* sheds a little light on the often overlooked social and employment struggles faced by individuals on the autism spectrum. Through the personal stories, insights, and research presented in this book, we hope to foster a deeper understanding and empathy toward the unique challenges of forming and maintaining friendships. By promoting awareness and acceptance, we hope to create a more supportive environment where autistic individuals are empowered to build meaningful connections. Our hope is that as we strive to transform echoes of isolation into harmonious bonds of friendship, we can all ensure that no one needs to feel alone on their journey.

HIM: IDEAS FOR COMMUNITY: 'There are very, very few autistic communities for people like us, though I'm aware of some projects developing in this arena. I laugh at this actually, because most of us don't connect well anyway, and truly are loners; more comfortable alone than with others. What would a community for us 'look like' or 'feel like?' How would that function? I must admit, I would want my family to be there with me. We need blended awareness in a community, along with our comfort people, our navigators, those we've learned to trust and be comfortable with.

IDEAS FOR WORK: I've tried to find my way, and work on a skill to contribute to society. I don't fit in. I did fairly well in the military as a weather observer because I was in the middle-of-nowhere Texas in a tower, watching clouds, and sometimes a tornado, go by.

Would it be possible to help us discover our *best* talents, our *focused* talents, and help us hone *those* skills into viable community resources? I believe we could do *so* much more than work on an assembly line. I may take a little longer to train, but my laser focus on the skill I'm good at, or hyper-interested in, would rarely wane. What an asset that could be!

For some reason, my son has been given many of the same challenges that I have. I'm sad about that. However, he has a welding certificate. He won't be able to work a traditional job, but what kind of a job is there for a young man like him? I don't want him to feel like he's squandered a sixty-year life in a small room playing computer games because the world didn't know how to allow him to contribute the one skill he has. And he is lost and confused because he doesn't know how to access any of the potential training available in the community beyond what he's already accomplished. What is there, for Ben?

POSTLUDE

HER: I have been down so many emotionally vulnerable and painful roads. He doesn't understand the emotional struggle that has kept us together yet meant the death of my myth-reality. He'll never know what it took to make the decision to remain married, as opposed to having the spouse I thought I would spend my life with. In my new reality, he is someone I enjoy, yet it is so difficult that I need significant breaks for self-care and down time. I have a long-term friend, approaching twenty-six years, but I do not have an equal partner.

I have found that those who have been hardest to interact with and been so incredibly difficult to handle, have been the ones who've given me the greatest opportunity for personal growth and development. I have found my values strengthened and patience increased exponentially when working with (yes, sometimes I say 'handle') my autistic family. I have not enjoyed some of the journey. It's been more difficult than I could have ever imagined. I've suffered my deepest loneliness and learned some of my deepest wisdom as I slogged through the trenches with those who needed me most.

I do give thanks to my family, from the gifted to the ultimately challenged, for the Kaleidoscope of Beauty I see in my life. Each of you are a lens through which I have found myriads of both joy and wonder.

Thank you for teaching me.

Essential Oils and Why We Use Them

We love essential oils. We use them extensively in our home; in diffusers, on jewelry, on our sheets, on our bodies and in our food.

Why? Have you ever felt like your food was magic? Thinking: 'Whoa! That food felt so good, so healthy,' when you eat your favorite salad, or drink a smoothie? Did it give you energy or clear your mind? The green in that food contains something called chlorophyll. It is remarkably suited to helping our bodies heal. At the very center of a plant's chlorophyll molecule is an atom of magnesium. At the very center of a human's hemoglobin molecule is iron. The remaining atoms found in those molecules are nearly identical. Your amazing body, when it consumes green food, instantly recognizes the nutritional building blocks and can immediately pull what it needs from the food in order to support your body systems.

I've shared a diagram for your reference.

Best Wishes,
Diana Catlin

"Unlock Well-Being"

For further information:
referral.doterra.me/130828

POSTLUDE

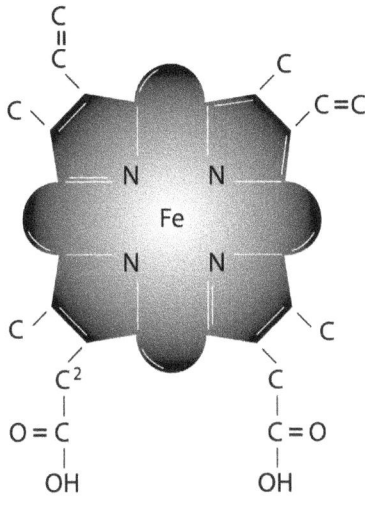

Human Blood Hemoglobin

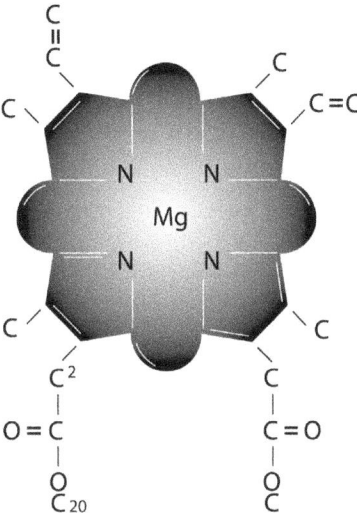

Plant Chlorophyll

ABOUT THE AUTHOR

Diana Catlin is a proud mother of nine whose parenting journey has been shaped by the various strengths of her neurodivergent family. With decades of experience, she's learned to embrace the beauty of individuality.

Whether through writing, genealogy research, or time with her grandchildren, Diana is driven by a deep love of connection and a passion for celebrating life's unique paths.

www.ingramcontent.com/pod-product-compliance
Lightning Source LLC
Chambersburg PA
CBHW052032030426
42337CB00027B/4970